To the
Gallaghers.
With best wishes

Artists & Writers
N. Y. C.

SNOOT IF YOU MUST

SNOOT IF YOU MUST

By LUCIUS BEEBE

Drawings by REA IRVIN

D. APPLETON-CENTURY COMPANY
INCORPORATED
NEW YORK   LONDON

Copyright, 1943, by

D. Appleton-Century Company, Inc.

FOR
CHUCK CLEGG
TO MAKE HIM LAUGH

GRATEFUL ACKNOWLEDGMENT is made to the editors and proprietors of *The American Mercury*, *Cosmopolitan* and the New York *Herald Tribune* for permission to reprint in this book certain excerpts from their columns.

L. B.

FOREWORD

WHEN the author of the farrago of confusions which constitutes the editorial economy of this book undertook the project, it was against the advice of the soundest minds in Bleeck's saloon, who greeted the intelligence that he was reopening the word foundry with loud shouts of

vii

"Phooey," "Don't be a dope," and "Have a touch of medicinal rock and rye and you'll be all right in a jiffy!"

"The guy has delusions," explained Ann Honeycutt to a new barkeep, who was reaching for a loaded ball bat in case the customer got really out of hand. "Last week when the sun was shining brightly for everyone else, he was having private rain!"

The content of the ensuing nonesuch, the dominant motive for the compilation of which is the author's low avarice and devotion to the United States mint, is nothing more than a catalogue of gleanings and vaporings vaguely related to life in New York and other urban midsts of the land. Some few of them have been culled, in their basis at least, from the syndicated column which kind employers, against their better judgment, have allowed the writer for some years to conduct in the New York *Herald Tribune* and elsewhere; some have been plucked out of what is sometimes known as thin air, a murk which in Manhattan is reported to contain in suspension more particles of debris, soot, hanging participles, counterfeit epigrams and microscopic fragments of ground glass than anywhere else on earth.

It has long been the contention of right-minded folk that the sole associates of the author were drunken printers, bogus grand dukes and the more pretentious of the town's hallroom boys; that his social discernment was on a level only slightly lower than the visual perceptions of an inmate of the Perkins Institute for the Blind, and that his way of life would end in nothing good. There can be no denying these indictments. They stand in the record, proudly engrossed and imperishable.

In defense of them, however, it may be remarked that you don't go to the circus with Dean Inge for company; that what is subversive to-day will almost certainly be patriotic to-morrow, and that, since the way of life of the entire world has ended in nothing good, who is the author to stand in the way of a universal progress toward perdition?

Now and then, too, in the professional life of every paragrapher, someone arises in meeting to question, not so much the veracity or good faith of the fellow, as the strict degree of accuracy characteristic of his anecdotes. Not so long ago an even-tempered but skeptical editorialist on the staff of the *Saturday Review of Literature* commenting on some more or less preposterous antic chronicled by the author, inquired: "Why do things like that happen only when this fellow Beebe is around?"

There are several answers to this well-mannered eyebrow-raising. The first is that this writer is employed as a professional connoisseur of fatuities, and another is that he doesn't have to be on the premises when the overt incident occurs, but that, since it is his business, he is more likely to be there than a less casual observer of the Manhattan comedy, just as a fireman is more apt to be at hand when the roof falls in than is the reader of the next morning's breakfast-table editions. Associate with fancy comics, and you encounter fancy and comic circumstances.

It was actually within six feet of the author's table at the Metropolitan Opera that Richard Knight performed his celebrated handstands. Valentina Schlee was his luncheon guest at Jack and Charlie's when she made her famous crack about the cheap availability of mink coats: "Meenk, meenk? Meenk, it is for footballs games!" He was personally within calling distance when Virginia Faulkner presented a taxi driver who was complaining about social injustice some years ago in midnight Fifty-second Street with a tidy firkin of paté de foie gras. He was on duty for the city desk in 1934 at the fanciest and most utterly Bedlamite flag-raising within recent memory, when Gertrude Stein's *Four Saints in Three Acts* had its outrageous première at the Avery Memorial in Hartford. He was on hand at City Hall on the occasion when Mayor Walker, in a moment of confusion, made a welcome-to-the-city speech to Gerhart Hauptmann, the dramatist, hailing him as a great German industrialist. He was present *in propria persona* when the majordomo of a certain Fifth Avenue dowager, whose triplex flat was so large that she had never explored it, announced that luncheon was served in the Elizabethan Salon, or whatever, and she inquired, quite ingenuously: "Where is it?" Get around enough in this town, and life is pretty much a succession of gags and drawings out of the *New Yorker,* most of them in the more troglodyte moments of James Thurber. But whether one prefers his Manhattan in terms of Thurber, Peter Arno or William Saroyan, no observer in what he may choose to call with a guffaw his right mind will undertake to depict it in overtones of wholly rational conduct.

The late Odd McIntyre, master of all New York paragraphers, in his latter years when this department

knew and sometimes contributed to him, worked on
a slightly different basis. Toward the end he didn't get
around so much in person, and therefore he tailored his
goods to a pattern of established clichés, editorially
speaking. His copy was full of bankrupted brokers leap-
ing from cornices after the market crash. He probably
was, in fancy, witness to more Chinese hatchet murders
than exist in all the tong-war records. Every one who
wore a top hat was, for him, a partner in the House of
Morgan. It gratified the gaudiest expectations of his
customers in suburbia and tickled local readers by establishing the legend that Gotham was really Babylon in
an opera cloak.

With people going crazier by the minute, you have
only to step outside the door of the Stork Club to encounter a scheme of things so loony that Count Screw-
loose of Toulouse would climb back into the madhouse
even faster than he used to do in Milt Gross's wonderful
cartoon by that name, with loud screams to his little
dog: "Iggy, keep an eye on me!"

The life slogan of the author's favorite friend, to
whom this index of infamies is inscribed, is "What of
it?" The title which appears on the jacket is no more
than a paraphrase of this sentiment.

L. B.

CONTENTS

xiv   CONTENTS

ILLUSTRATIONS

1

GLOBALONEY GOLCONDA

MORE than any other single factor responsible for the established suburban attitude that New York is sheer heaven to visit once a year but that gold couldn't hire any one in his right mind to live there, is a perfectly well-founded suspicion that the screaming and roaring into which strangers within Manhattan's gates plunge themselves when on the town is a constant state of affairs. In saner communities business is not accomplished in the fine Scotch mist that envelops every sort of professional or commercial transaction in Babylon-on-the-Make, and the outlander is frightened out of his wits at the spectacle of people achieving their affairs in an atmosphere which in his mind is associated only with extravagant whoopdedo. Save in Hollywood, professional careers aren't achieved elsewhere in a prevailing midst of night clubs, gin palaces, and crazy luxe. Business is business and fun is fun, but to shake the two up together with just a dash of absinthe tends to unhinge the minds of out-of-towners.

To the Manhattanite who is going places and getting

the business of living done to its maximum capacity, this, of course, is the most compelling fascination of the urban scene, but the urgency, the selective evolution, and comparative efficiency of existence here terrify the leisurely fellow from other locales, where, metaphorically speaking, the breadfruit grows more abundantly and prestige can be established by less spacious gestures.

Encountered at a high-pressure cocktail shebang was a highly successful young barrister from Boston, who, in his home town, is considered a very sufficient fellow. He watched the scene, which was populated entirely with celebrities and professional folk going about their daily business of contacts, flattery, social intrigue, character-scuttling, and generally getting somewhere, and then ingenuously commented: "But all these people seem to want something from each other!" Of course, they want something from each other, which is the whole secret of life in New York, and their lives are predicated on the business of getting the particular something each one wants. That's why the professional, social, and business successes of New Yorkers are the ranking successes of the world, and it's also why the city's Latinate motto might very well be changed to "Nut'in' for Nut'in'."

This urgency, combined with absorbing alcohol for business reasons and consummating deals of presumably vast military moment at the St. Regis bar, is in no way abated by the circumstance of war; only its terms are changed with the times. Most of the props and the house staff are the same as they were during the happy days when the Hotsy-Totsy shootings and the ventilations of various gentry at the Club Abbey by Dutch Schultz and Legs Diamond were the closest approach to military en-

counters known. A few of the veteran actors still play
the rôles they created at the Beaux Arts Balls and ringside tables in the Little Club or the old Plaza (or Connie Bennett) Grill, but the younger players have
changed with the times, and the Hall-room Boys of Lexington and Madison Avenues are in road companies in
North Africa, Australia, or the Savoy Bar in London.

Indeed, it is remarkable how few of the established
landmarks of hurrah so widely publicized by the wolf
packs of pre-war café society has disappeared. John Perona's El Morocco, the Stork, Monte Carlo Beach are
still the dominant after-midnight saloons, while the
Plaza, the St. Regis, the Colony, the Coq Rouge, the
Savoy Plaza, Jack and Charlie's, and a handful of others
stand fast as the restaurants of costly fashion, some of
them with cabaret or night-club overtones on the side.

But the change in personnel was most articulately
noted by Alva Johnston in mid-1943 when he returned
to his native haunts after more than a year spent, mostly,
in the County Strip, Hollywood. He was leaning against
the bar at "21" exchanging Martinis and bitcheries with
the writer, when he looked over the sea of new faces,
half of them second lieutenants and remarked: "Holy
Christ, I don't know a person in the house. Society must
be coming back!" Alva was neither the first nor the last
person to be impressed profanely by the new order in
the saloons.

With Ulysses away at the wars a very curious army of
suitors descended on the boulevards to woo the town's
headwaiter Penelopes. There were rich French refugees
with manners which would have outraged a Colorado
mining-camp in gold-rush days. There were the camp

followers of the Federal government in Washington full of idealism about milk for the Hottentots and more practical visions of champagne for themselves, and there were members of the armed forces from Elko, Nevada, and Cedar Rapids, Iowa, who had always hoped to see New York and be shoved around in the Astor Bar but had never dreamed of doing it at the expense of the taxpayers. And super-added were regiments of shipyard workers and war contract hands and their wives, who, having filled the front parlor with enough Grand Rapids furniture to stock Sears Roebuck for a decade and still having money to spend, had decided to see where Miss Beth Leary had lunch and order the same things, only twice as much of them. There was a great boom in fancy mixed drinks which old-stand barkeeps, accustomed to the whisky sling preferences of the café crowd, hadn't been called on to compound in years. Arnold Reuben ordered in approximately a hundred gross of rag dolls and floppy calico kittens of the kind esteemed as the last word in fashionable interior décor when draped around fringed piano lamps in Oklahoma City.

Amid these strange manifestations of revolution there tottered a few bemused New Yorkers, shufflers in a dank saraband of lost causes. Averell Harriman wore a glazed look at lunchtime at the Colony. Dorothy Kilgallen admittedly rated pickpockets and racetrack touts in her columns as the old nobility of the town so long as they had a police record as far back as 1938. Carino, emir of maîtres d'hôtel, considered opium pipes and having beautiful pipe dreams which included the Vincent Astors at their regular table at El Morocco and customers who didn't add the word "wine" when they ordered a hodful of champagne. Harold Ross of the *New Yorker,* feeling that local landmarks were passing rapidly, took a vow never to have replaced the missing front tooth which for years he had intended to have fixed but which had become a celebrated sight for the tourist trade. Charlie Norris, around for a few days from San Francisco to sign a contract with his publishers, found Gotham funnier than ever and expressed a whim to write a contemporary portrait of the city to be called *Globaloney Goldrush,* a title based on the celebrated word minting of Mrs. Henry Luce, the Connecticut congresswoman.

One of the stranger manifestations of the times was the status of film actors, usually and in normal times considered by the judicious pretty spurious currency, the professional equivalent of a Confederate banknote, and given a brisk brusheroo by all but night-club proprietors and tabloid columnists. In raging times of peace perhaps the saddest of all fish out of water in the big town was the parvenu film celebrity off the reservation, who was on Manhattan safari to make personal appearances when one of his pictures opened, or merely hell-bent for hiccups where neither Will Hays nor his manager could clap restraining hands on him. Nine times out of ten everything he did was wrong; every gesture in which he indulged assumed a cachet of the phony, and if he tried to put on the dog in the manner with which he was accustomed to impress and fascinate the peasants of Santa Monica and Beverly Hills, he got the horse laugh especially reserved by waiter captains for practitioners of spurious hauteur. The reason for this was, of course, that in other towns, especially on the home grounds, his elegances stacked up pretty favorably with the local notions of bon ton, but when he hit Manhattan he suddenly found himself up to the neck in the sort of life and people he had been counterfeiting for a living, and

No longer the saddest fish

suffered a consequent rush of discomfort and embarrassed inferiority to the head.

To offset this, unless he was experienced and could exercise an unaccustomed restraint, he was likely to indulge a suppressed penchant for the grand manner, which usually set on him with all the authenticity of a top hat on a Sioux. He tried being uppish with maîtres d'hôtel and found himself lodged behind potted palms in the kitchen alleyway for his pains. He stood in the white lights of Forty-fifth Street inviting the attention, abhorrent to the judicious, of the autograph fans, and made a public clown of himself. His press agent announced his arrival to city editors and his gracious willingness to chat with reporters, but since he had nothing of any conceivable interest to say, he was deluged with neglect. Finally, he got falling-down drunk, and, to compensate his fury of frustration, contrived to insinuate himself into a hideous brawl at the Stork Club which made it necessary for him to leave town the next day in a snowstorm of denials, accusations, and protestations of outraged innocence which fooled nobody. Sneaking into Los Angeles behind drawn curtains and with terror in his heart, since there had been a specific clause in his contract stipulating no fist fighting in the Stork Club, he confided to his friends that New York was a dreadful place and entirely populated with exhibitionists, phonies, dubious celebrities, and surly drunks.

But the wars changed all that, and, for a time, anyway, the Hollywood ham found himself in almost as much demand as Kansas City beefsteak. His presence was more than tolerated, it was cultivated by the strange new faces who, most of them, had never been in a legitimate theater in their lives and who actually believed a film player to be an actor.

The reaction of certified New Yorkers to all this was at first one of superciliousness, then one of terror, and, finally, the adoption of defense measures. Old patroons, their residence in Park Avenue dating back to the legendary days of 1929 and even earlier, organized them-

selves to give battle, and its first manifestation was a
movement of secrecy to protect and cherish local institutions from the solvent hordes of invaders. Is an as
yet unexploited restaurant of fair repute discovered and
approved? Keep it a secret! Has that nice old Joe Doax,
who used to be behind the bar at the Barberry Room
and knows everybody worth knowing, got a place of his
own? Don't let anybody but the right people know, and
perhaps we can keep the rich refugees away for a while,
anyway. Voyagers abroad in the opulent twenties still
recall the unholy raptures of the American tourist who
discovered "a little place where only the real French
people go and the cooking is the authentic French thing.
They hate foreigners there!" In New York in 1943 the
watchword was the precise reverse, and it was a heroic
Balboa of the bistros who unearthed a "little place
where only real New Yorkers go and there isn't a
Frenchman in the joint."

The great battle against change in New York is likely
to see its turning point and ultimate victory for the
established institutions when the armed services return
from the hemispheres where global strategy has sent
them, for not even the natives enslaved by the occupying
invaders are fiercer in their determination to maintain
every imaginable trace of its pre-war civilization than
are its exiles in New Caledonia and Guadalcanal,
Tunisia and the Strand. The business of glamour, living up to Cecil B. De Mille's notions of life in Babylon-
on-the-Hudson, has taken a considerable licking since
the outbreak of open hostilities, but there are still a
few residuary traces of the wonders that bugged the eyes
of Odd McIntyre's readers and supplied Fannie Hurst,

Katharine Brush, and other novelists with glitter copy. That modern warfare isn't glamorous is an obvious truism, and that it is only proper for those not actively engaged in combat to abate their way of life, even if they can still afford it, is equally patent, but that a certain amount of swish, swank, and swelling around is justified and really desired by the men away at the wars is apparent to any one with any appreciable correspondence with service men.

Nine out of ten letters received by the author of this volume in his capacity as a syndicated newspaper columnist, whether from personal acquaintances or strangers in Africa or the islands or Texas training camps, want to know about the fripperies and foolishness of the town. They want clippings from Winchell, Kilgallen and Sobol and the *New Yorker,* and they want to hear about food and drinking and theaters and night life. That these aspects of urban existence should be diminished, blacked out, or subject to attacks, always in the name of patriotism and expediency, by snouters and bluenoses, seems to sadden them.

They want the town to be as they always knew or imagined it, not a lean-faced and parochial metropolitan crossroads, and they want some assurance that when they get back there will still be the things in which they once took pleasure—first nights and leg shows and tinsel night clubs and steak houses on Broadway and motor-cars covered with gimcrack plumbing and foolish hats on girls and dates under the clock at the Biltmore, and Roselands and Stork Clubs and Madison Square Gardens all over. Not only, it is safe to guess, will they be unhappy if they return to find familiar things missing;

they'll be good and cross at people who did away with them or let them slide.

The letters from the young men at arms in far places vary from the profane to the sentimental and from the informed to rustic naïveté, but they all express an almost pathetic hanker for the good old days and the implicit belief that change in almost any form is betrayal.

"What we want most to find when we get home," writes a technical sergeant from Callan in California, "is not the bright new world full of such sentimental piffle as we hear from the global humanitarians and other crackpots in high places. We want everything just as we left it, imperfections and all. As other soldiers seem to have written in to you, we're going to do some very drastic things about it if we come back to find that a lot of imbecile 'reforms,' like prohibition in the last war, have been put over on us in our absence. Just leave well enough alone at home is all we ask!"

"I've never been to New York," writes a first-class seaman from the receiving base at San Diego, "but it's the first place I'm going to head for when I get a chance, and I want everything just as I've always read about it and as I bet a million sailors, if there are that many, dream of it. The picture of the greatest city in the world with no auto traffic and blackouts and restrictions of all sorts is almost as bad news as a major military disaster would be. Gloom on the home front to men in service is just as depressing as bad news from the fighting fronts must be to people at home, and if food shortages, liquor shortages, curfews, and the like aren't bad news, I don't know what is!"

These are perhaps only samples of the sentiments of worldly and carnal-minded fellows writing to a worldly and carnal-minded reporter, but there seems to be quite an abundance of them, and most of them are profane and emphatic in their sentiments. The correspondent who writes to suggest that the four freedoms be enlarged to include free beer and free lunch may be of a strictly practical mind and maybe a depraved fellow of the baser sort, but he's not unrepresentative.

2

THE COVERED WAGON FOLLIES

ONE of the first by-products of the latter thirties to disappear amid the greater urgencies of the wars was a spacious gesture of promotion which had become more or less conventional and incidental to the launching of any motion-picture enterprise of special pretentiousness.

The evolution of the film junket may well engage the attentions of scholarly research, but in general it had its origins in the blowsy and search-light illuminated super premières of a more naïve Hollywood era, passed into a stage characterized by chamber of commerce Morris dancing in a locale pertinent, within the imagining of press-agents at least, to the film's content, had its by-product in plushy receptions in the Waldorf-Astoria and minor traffic disturbances in Times Square, and found its final and most magnificent flowering in the de luxe overland pilgrimage to some geographically improbable point, into which trainloads of stars from the west coast and reporters from the citadels of the east were gently and alcoholically decanted by train, plane, and motor caravan. The last of these magnificences is recommended to students of the civilization along with débutante parties, American Legion conventions, and Tammany outings.

It was an elegant and gratuitous folly, framed at great cost for the flattery and befuddlement of newspaper folk and the astonishment of the natives of whatever community was happily singled out for the massacre. Probably it was actually good promotion for the celluloid masterpiece being launched, but that was a consideration which had no weight with any one concerned, let alone the film companies. There are those who will miss it and cling to the pious hope that they may live to see the film junket revived, not only in all its former glory, but with the latest modern improvements within the gift of science and industry.

The grand gala junket was usually accomplished through the agency of de luxe private trains in two sections and converging from New York and Hollywood upon a predetermined objective. Every other car was a bar car, frontier shack, dance hall, gambling hell, or refreshment oasis run on a twenty-four hour basis, and in addition to the legitimate feature writers, Frank Farrell, Howard Barnes, John Chapman, Hedda Hopper, Kate Cameron, Bill Boehnel *et al.*, there was usually a miscellany of gilded camp followers quite unassociated with the film in hand, such as Bruce Cabot, then in the employ of a rival studio, who turned up at Warner Brothers' *Virginia City* hollering, and Jack Kriendler, the squire of Jack and Charlie's, who is practically a national ambassador of good will and who hasn't missed a cowboy party since the first year of the wonderful San Francisco World's Fair.

If the film was first shown to a breathless world at such a place as Dodge City, located in driest Kansas, fantastic quantities of refreshments accompanied the celebrants across the countryside. If otherwise, they were sluiced and replenished at convenient water stops. Roulette concessionaires bid for rights on the more pretentious cross-country hauls, and at Reno, on one occasion, Warner Brothers actually supplied correspondents with an initial stake in silver dollars with which to commence operations against the town's swindle syndicates.

Not all the covered wagon follies were as exquisitely planned or as comfortably mounted as, say, *Santa Fe Trail* or *Knute Rockne, All American.* The *Gone with the Wind* opening at Atlanta, while achieving a monstrous success in publicity, ran afoul of a convention of learned medicos who had taken over the town's hotels, and there simply weren't any beds. *Virginia City* and *Union Pacific* were the most thunderous of all film overtures, and newspapers and press associations covered their every angle, and highly salaried feature reporters filed thousands of words of telegraph stories on their more colorful and sanguinary aspects. These epic confusions stirred the populace of entire states to dionysiac frenzies, as any one will recall who was present when 400,000 Nebraskans hungry for holiday and attired by a munificent municipality in plug hats and crinolines descended, for four gun-toting days, on Omaha, to share the bounty of the Union Pacific Railroad and Paramount Pictures when that deathless saga of the high iron, *Union Pacific*, was unveiled.

Probably the *Union Pacific* spike-laying was the most epic launching in the history of films, because it involved the geniuses of two of the greatest showmen of their age, William M. Jeffers, President of the Union Pacific Railroad, and Cecil B. De Mille of Paramount, who had directed and produced the screen story of frontier conquest. Abetting their efforts at promotion were the entire resources of the State of Nebraska, the city of Omaha, and a corps of high-pressure barkers in the employ of all concerned. The only thing missing was the Vatican Choir accompanied by the Gloria Trumpeters, and, given time, Steve Hannagan might have secured their services too.

As the home office of the Union Pacific Railroad, Omaha, otherwise a town of negligible social aspects and accommodations, was the logical jumping-off place for the baptism of Paramount's heroic film of the six-shooting sixties, but most of the State of Nebraska, which had been neglected by the circus and other accustomed carnivals for several years and was ripe for super-dooper doings, to the extent of 400,000 persons, dug up grandfather's Sharps rifle and tooled to town for a spot of whisky and gunfire.

The better to recreate the period of the film, Omaha, under the guidance of a first citizen and local patriot, named Otto Swanson, with an acknowledged capacity for fancy frivolities second to none, undertook a series of dinners, luncheons, receptions, fêtes champêtres, and covered wagon parades on a scale to make the annual Rodeo at neighboring Cheyenne look to its laurels.

False fronts were erected on most of the buildings in the principal streets and made brave with advertising archaisms and period decorations. Ancient slogans appeared in soap lettering on the mirrors of the local saloons, and rondo-coolo and chuckaluck games flourished in every pool parlor. More than twenty thousand frock coats of exciting pattern, crinoline dresses, sunbonnets, lavender plug hats, and other festival garments were imported from a Chicago mail-order house and distributed at cost in the interest of municipal solidarity, for, as psychologists are well aware, there is nothing so provocative of fancy manners as fancy attire.

As was the custom at all such slightly inspired frontier promotion convocations, every known variety of whiskers was encouraged. Mutton chops, Mormon fringes, burnsides, spade beards, imperials, gold-rush alfalfas, vandykes, handlebar mustachios appeared on barkeepers, messenger boys, police braves, firemen, hotel clerks, and otherwise sober bank tellers and hotel executives. Sobriety in its less academic sense was at a considerable discount, and Omaha maintained a mild but none-the-less perceptible state of glow for four days straight. There were crises induced by runaway horses, the accidental firing of business premises and beards, and the occasional shooting of a participant, excitements which were taken as a matter of course by all concerned except the victims of gunfire, who could only infrequently be induced to view their wounds in the light of clean fun.

Both De Mille and Jeffers were and are expert showmen, and in Omaha the overlords of steel and celluloid slugged it out toe to toe, in a manner to make the rival bids for photographic attention at opera openings of Mrs. George Washington Cavanaugh and Mrs. Cornelius Vanderbilt seem the merest love taps. Romancing the cameramen was carried to a fine flower of perfection, and, as both moguls were in command of extensive corps of their own staff photographers, the flicker of speed guns was as heat lightning of an August evening.

At the classic ceremonial dinner given at this latterday Field of the Cloth of Gold, De Mille and Jeffers sat in consular state at a head table which overflowed with fruits of earth, flasks of Wilkens Family, and partially concealed Remington derringers. Dr. D. M. Nigro, a locally prominent sawbones and follower of Hippocrates, who distributed business cards among the revelers engrossed with his professional phone number and the legend GUNSHOT WOUNDS A SPECIALTY was attired in a green Prince Albert, canary Ascot tie, and stovepipe hat of white beaver and consuming drinking arrangements known as Frontier Slings at the bar. In the course of the evening there were accidents and victims of vertigo, thrown bottles, or just plain falling down to be treated by the most ornamental medico west of the Mississippi. At the press table, immediately in front of the speaker's dais, were ranked Terry DeLapp, Bob Gilham, and a number of high-power publicists, including Bill Hebert, De Mille's personal herald, who were engaged in quoting Proust, Swinburne, and Frank Ward O'Malley. Hebert had been presented by the grateful city fathers of Omaha with a Colt's Frontier Model peacemaker, a single-action wallpiece of vintage design which was swinging in his hand in an arc so that its potential line of fire embraced most of the guests at the head table. Since the stock of blank cartridges in Omaha had long since been exhausted and there was an even chance that any ornamental firearms in sight might be

Fancy attire stimulated fancy manners

charged with ball ammunition, Jeffers, as the sights swung past his hastily averted gaze, was not unreasonably perturbed and sent a messenger down with word that he would be very much upset indeed if Hebert should discharge the weapon in his direction. De Mille overheard the conversation and immediately rose to the occasion.

"Excuse me, Mr. Jeffers," he said, "but Mr. Hebert works for me, and I rather imagine he's pointing that mangonel in my direction!"

"Indeed not, sir," countered Jeffers. "He's my guest, and I insist that he is leveling that hackbut at me!"

"I take it as a point of courtesy that my staff always train their calivers at me during state dinners," snapped De Mille.

"He'll lay that escopet at me or I'll know the reason why," snarled Jeffers with his most terrible snarl.

At that moment the problem of protocol was solved as the musketoon exploded with a frightening detonation, blowing an appreciable hole in the ballroom floor and scaring Hebert out of his wits. Both Jeffers and De Mille were gratified at the outcome and made long speeches in praise of each other.

One of the last occasions at which great numbers of railroad presidents converged from the corners of the continent in their private Pullmans, the opening of *Union Pacific,* was dominated by the arrival from Chicago over the tracks of the Illinois Central of a train of seventeen private cars assembled for the occasion and run at the order of W. Averell Harriman, chairman of the board of the Union Pacific Railroad.

It required less than a decade to perfect the technic of christening film spectacles through the agency of geographic hurrah, and by the time such interstate tumults had to be abated in the general interest, it had been brought to a state where the structural basis, which, of course, was alcohol and locomotion, possessed scant possibilities for improvement. In the case of *Virginia City* the executives of Warner Brothers frankly went on

record to the effect that they were curious to know just
how much money could be spent on this type of promotion and instructed their various vicars that there
was no limit on their fancy in the way of disbursements.
The result was that, weeks in advance, New York and
Hollywood film and feature reporters and syndicate
managers were canvassed in the interest of determining
the types of cigarettes, champagne, and mineral waters
they liked best and other conveniences theretofore
largely confined to the pleasuring of Indian potentates
and partners in the House of Morgan.

There was invariably a certain amount of blood-
shed, mayhem, and incidental injury to the participant
in these forays. It was on board the Warner Brothers'
Special westbound out of Chicago over the trackage of
the Chicago and North Western Railway that Humphrey
Bogart met with an accident of more than passing curiosity when, drinking highballs with Thornton Dele-
hanty and Big Boy Williams on the observation plat-
form of their train, he had occasion to dispose of an
empty glass without troubling to ring for the porter.
The special was then rolling across the midnight wastes
of Iowa, and there wasn't a chance of a tossed beaker
hitting anything, but Bogart, to make sure of not encountering an oncoming train on the parallel track,
carefully hurled the glass into the night off the right-
hand side of the platform, confident that the only thing
along the right of way at that point was a ditch and
telegraph poles. The glass, in a million pieces and at
astonishing velocity, was instanter returned in the faces
of the group of thirsty passengers, doing some damage
to the assembled and valuable film profiles. It had

bounced off the smoke box of a speeding locomotive headed in the opposite direction. Bogart had failed to realize that the North Western was, and is, the only railroad in the United States regularly maintaining left-hand operations as is the rule in English traffic, and that trains headed in reverse directions pass each other on the right-hand side. It was easily the most expansive gesture of its kind.

Whether or not Warner Brothers selected the script of *Virginia City* solely with an eye to the possibilities of a junket in the frontier reaches of Nevada may be open to dispute. The film itself was of very little consequence, but it has always been accepted in advertising circles that the less meritorious the product the more magnificent the promotion required to put it over, and, on this basis, *Virginia City* was very low-grade ore indeed.

No other vicinage, however, was so calculated to offer the celebrants at a barn-raising the opportunities for untrammeled personal endeavor and inventiveness supplied in the High Sierras by Reno town and Virginia City itself. Notoriously addicted to ringin' and swingin' 'em, high, wide, and fancy during 365 days and nights a year, Reno got itself into unusually fancy costume and went to no end of trouble to see to it that pilgrims to the first showing of Warner Brothers' deathless epic felt practically no pain at all during the time of their stay.

Thirty-odd Pullmans of thirsty, solvent, and determined first nighters, most of them names of consequence and all of them right handy folk with bottles, poker chips, and ballad music, were an invasion not to be taken casually. There were also forty or fifty thousand camp followers, cow hands, and autograph collectors to reckon with, and Jack Fuggert, the slot-machine king, and the proprietors of the Bank Club, the Town House, the Dog House, and other assorted casinos and temples of what is known with a snicker as chance, brightened visibly as the Southern Pacific's specials rolled in from Los Angeles, San Francisco, and Chicago. Top hats and frock coats blossomed on every hand, and the night was glad with laughter and playing on stringed instruments.

First to arrive and very likely the last to go was handsome and amiable Bruce Cabot, who arrived in a flying machine a full day ahead of time, was made a member of the police department by Chief Andy M. Welliver, changed to frontier attire and was in the Bank Club in a kitchen midden of roulette chips within an hour. Although not implicated in the film itself, Mr. Cabot was probably the favorite character of a dazzled and admiring audience and was patently Public Favorite No. 1 throughout the week end.

Humphrey Bogart, who actually acted in *Virginia City*, was also received with suitable glad cries and disorders, but since, whenever their appearance was solicited at receptions, in parades or other spectacles, Mr. Cabot contrived to insinuate himself between Mr. Bogart and his public, effectively masking him out with perhaps six inches of stature and proportionate breadth, any decibel count would have given Mr. Cabot the palm. Another scoundrelly device resorted to by Mr. Cabot was the circulation of a rumor that Mr. Bogart was giving away silver dollars with every autograph, a circumstance which, when it was definitely proved to be not so, tended to estrange Mr. Bogart's public.

The arrival from Los Angeles of the West Coast special, awash as it was with actors, executives, reporters, valets, barkeeps, guards, gunmen and professional junketeers was the high point of the week-end. As a train itself it was a thing of beauty, its consist, powered by one of the Espee's cab-first Mallets, including two restaurant cars, two bar cars, an observation lounge, fifteen private-room Pullmans, and two stall cars filled with mounts for the more determinedly Western actors. The bar car was the one that saw service the year before at the opening of *Dodge City* and resplendent with cut glass and crystal chandeliers, frontier souvenirs, and a barroom nude reclining graciously in oils above the bar and miraculously endowed with an undulant stomach to give the effect of breathing. Throughout the week the bar and restaurant cars maintained day and night service, and it was possible for those who temporarily assumed inanimate postures on the floor at any hour of the twenty-four to rise again and renew their labors at the expense of the hospitable Warner Brothers.

Of all the celebrities present, certainly the most magnificently accoutered was that old rider of the Fifty-second Street ranges, Two Trigger Jack Kriendler. Mr. Kriendler required two entire drawing rooms for his wardrobe and made no fewer than ten complete changes during the thirty hours the special was on the Reno siding. Hailed by the populace as a film star of uncertain identity but undoubted splendor, Mr. Kriendler was unwilling to betray this public trust and graciously consented to rise and take a bow whenever Errol Flynn,

Gilbert Roland, or Tom Mix was called for. He was also agreeable to footing enormous drink bills at the Bank Club or Riverside and seldom lacked a following that would gladly have nominated him for governor or even president had the occasion demanded.

Virginia City itself, twenty-five miles up in the mountains and seat of the fortunes of the bonanza kings, Fair, Mackay, Flood, and a host of others, was achieved Saturday afternoon by the entire company packed into fifteen huge buses and guided by a score or so of motorcycle outriders. Allegedly the expedition was undertaken for the first showing of *Virginia City* in film form, but so straitened were the confines of the local theater that it became something more in the nature of a pious pilgrimage to the famed Crystal Bar, the most splendid oasis in all the surrounding countryside and a museum of the years when the Comstock Lode produced some $700,000,000 worth of ore and created millionaires by the hundred, whose mansions rose as testaments to their worth from Fifth Avenue to Telegraph Hill.

The Crystal's name derives from its chandeliers, which are miracles of blue-and-white crystal, and from its multitude of decanters, punch-bowls, and assorted drinking utensils. Ten perspiring barkeeps found it difficult to assuage the thirst of the throngs which paraded in the dust of C Street, the town's main drag, and the overflow bulged the walls of the Bucket of Blood, the rival (but not original) Crystal Bar, Sawdust Corner, and the Orient. Drinks were cheap everywhere—two bits for highballs and a dime for a big beer—and stylish gentlemen in sideburns and gray top hats halted their two-seater buggies at the hitching posts and descended for a quick one while news cameras clicked and the people cheered. Up at Piper's Opera House an auction for the benefit of the New York Metropolitan Opera Fund was in progress. In the Western Union office, facing on the tumult, reporters in Albert watch-chains and cowboy scarves were filing copy between purely medicinal passes at flasks of redeye. There was a runaway outside the Wells Fargo office, and one of Mr. Bogart's admirers stole his best black sombrero. In a word, Virginia City lived up to all that the newsreel men had hoped for from it.

Reno that night was any man's town, and, while the actual numbers of visitors hardly topped the crowd on an average Saturday night in summer, its individual and collective solvency, according to Chief of Police Welliver, not to mention its index of absorbency and capacity for punishment, were of a most unusual order. As a matter of record it was generally estimated that the take of the principal gambling establishments of the town, not counting the slot machines, was somewhat in excess of $200,000. For all these carnival circumstances, Chief Welliver and his force were not overburdened save with occasional traffic problems. There are only two crimes on the statute books of Nevada: one is murder and the other the removal of currency or wealth in any form from within the confines of the state. The first, because of the good temper of the crowd, was vastly improbable, while the second, as any one familiar with roulette, faro, craps, and poker as played in Reno will agree, was utterly and completely impossible.

The social dictator of Reno's destinies is Virginia, the chief telephone operator at the Riverside Hotel. At any moment Virginia can tell any one of consequence where his next engagement is, what he should wear, and the whereabouts of all or any of his acquaintances, and Saturday evening found her celebrity service functioning at absolute capacity. Coöperating with Johnny Harkins, chief of protocol for Warner Brothers, with Hymie Fink, Hollywood's ranking news photographer and a mine of information about any midst in which he finds himself, and with a corps of tipsters and informants, Virginia was able to keep the situation as well in hand as any Saturday night in Reno ever will be.

It may be contended that the wild West and its local overtones of Comstock days was brought back to Reno and Virginia City through the agency of Warner Brothers' property department, the Bar B H Ranch, of Palm Springs, California; the chuck houses of Manhattan's Fifty-second Street, and Rodeo Ben, the cowboy tailor, whose general store is located in Philadelphia, and there will be a certain amount of truth in the contention. But it was a thorough job of recreating an exciting era and approximating its time spirit, and the survivors unanimously agreed that it was a catastrophe which they will willingly experience again the moment Warner Brothers dreams up a new period design film and starts sending out the invitations.

Another major convulsion in the sagebrush accompanied the inaugural of *Santa Fé Trail,* as a setting for which Warner Brothers, the State of New Mexico, and the Atchison, Topeka, and Santa Fé Railroad aptly enough selected the town of Santa Fé. Each was anxious to add its two or three hundred thousand dollars' worth of hospitality and conspired to make the rout one of whooping and abandon in which they were aided by the participants to the last gasp of their whisky breaths. That the whole three days' festivities took place during a howling New Mexican blizzard was a splendid excuse for being in the wrong saloons. There was imported every known device of fashionable Hollywood publicization, even down to the search-lights, and the ultimate comment on the whole fracas was spoken by a youthful carriage starter at the Fonda Hotel, who had been impervious to the comings and goings of Errol Flynn, Rudy Vallee, Wayne Morris, and Nancy Carroll. "Jeez," he said, "you know them search-lights is so powerful they'll set fire a haystack at a hundred yards!"

If any index of the success of the occasion was required, it was cited that quite a number of the invited guests actually got to see the screening of *Santa Fé Trail* itself, something which rarely if ever happened at such round-ups. From the bars of the Fonda to the Paris, Lensic, and Burro Alley Theaters was no more than a seltzer squirt, and Reginald Gardiner, Donald Crisp, Charles Ruggles, and Johnny Weismuller were able to make personal appearances with a minimum of pain and discomfort.

For the moment such six-reel rodeos are in eclipse, but one has only to consult the overlords of publicity and promotion in the studios of Hollywood and their Broadway offices to gather that, one of these fine days, there will again be junkets, of not merely trancontinental but positively cosmic proportions.

3

AT THE EMPIRE

IT was a pleasant flurry of sentimental searchings of heart among New Yorkers of landau and gas-lamp memories which was occasioned a few years since by the threat of destruction to the Empire Theatre. Now, to be sure, the danger is for the moment suspended, and systoles and diastoles that never ought to have been so dangerously agitated have returned to normal, but until the public mind was set at ease there were lavender-and-old-lace moments for many who had in the interim forgotten what part of the New York scene, how much at once a link and a souvenir of the past, the Empire really was. There have been too many desecrations of antiquity of late for the anticipation with anything but concern of the removal of the Empire.

The word antiquity is, of course, used only in the New York sense, meaning anything before yesterday or at most anything before the closing of Jack Dunstan's, for the Empire is only a little more than half a century old. But as such it constitutes a Manhattan landmark, dating from the blue days and fair previous to the third financial panic ago. Thus it becomes to the intelligence of the Empire State or Chrysler age something of an early Devonian, if not actually pre-Cambrian, relic.

The life span to date of the Empire has, in a manner of speaking, been precisely coincidental with an era of the greater American stage. At the time of the erection of the house in 1893, the golden age of tragedy on the American stage, the age of Booth, McCullough, Sr., and Barrett, had come to an end, and it was at the Empire that John Drew, Ethel Barrymore, William Gillette, Faversham and Maude Adams brought the new school to its flower and perfection. Thus the Empire is a monument not alone to a graceful and leisurely time spirit, epitomized by the glory that was the old Waldorf, the gaiety that was Rector's, but also to a notable tradition of play-acting as an art.

The doors of the Empire first opened to the general public on the evening of January 25, 1893, when the first ticket was handed to the attendant by George M. Pullman, president of the Pullman Palace Car Company, as a pass to see a performance of a military melodrama entitled *The Girl I Left Behind Me*. Al Hyman had laid the cornerstone of the house nine months previous and leased it to Charles Frohman with the remark that it was a "good site for a theater even though a little far uptown," and Frohman, delighted to have his own house for the first time, commissioned David Belasco and Frank Fyles, then the drama critic of the *Sun*, to write his first piece for him.

The house was opened with the pretty ceremony usual on such occasions. Mr. Belasco sat in a box and made a little speech during the first intermission; at the second, the crowd of distinguished first nighters made a concerted rush to the bar of Brown's chop house next door for the purpose of drinking success to the theater, and the final curtain was run down upon rapturous applause. It was considered a bit of a hardship to have to go out on to Broadway to get to the bar at Brown's, for that establishment when it was farther downtown had had a short passage built through into the lobby of Daly's, but everybody put up cheerfully with this primitive inconvenience, and the opening was considered an enormous success by all concerned.

The Girl I Left Behind Me was closely succeeded by a drama entitled *Liberty Hall,* which had its first performance in August, 1893, and whose cast included Henry Miller, Viola Allen, Cyril Scott, and Frank and Adolph Klauber.

Perhaps as much comment was attracted by the architectural style of the new Empire as by the house as a theatrical institution. The public prints of the times were filled with column-long accounts detailing the wainscoting of "pink Numidian marble, the glass ceiling illuminated by 150 electric light bulbs, the elaborate eighteen-foot fire-place, the very pretty archway in the balcony overlooking the foyer; the smoking room with its colors and effects representing [of all things] smoke, and the red crinkle silk Damascus drop curtain." Let not a less ingenuous generation, which leans toward glass, chromium, and straight lines, mock the naïve plush and splendor of the Empire, its smoke effects, its turkey carpets. They have endured long and pleasured many and will doubtless, if the hand of the wrecker is stayed, outlive all the improbable chairs and cock-eyed bookshelves ever devised by Salvador Dali in a mince-pie dream frenzy.

From the day it was opened onward it was apparent that the Empire was a New York institution. Most of the brilliant Frohman successes between 1893 and the

time when that producer sailed to his death on the last voyage of the *Lusitania* were produced there. Henry Miller, Viola Allen, and William Faversham played in *Sowing the Wind,* John Drew and Maude Adams in *Rosemary* and *Under the Red Robe,* Margaret Anglin and Charles Richman in *Mrs. Dane's Defence,* and Maude Adams appeared three hundred consecutive nights in *The Little Minister.* Later Ethel Barrymore, Billie Burke, William Gillette, Otis Skinner, Doris Keene, and Sarah Bernhardt played there. It was always a house with a distinguished cast listed in the electric bulbs on the roof.

Ever a house for the carriage patronage, even after Charles and the bays gave way to a Pope Hartford and the Pope Hartford to Rolls-Royces and expensive motors from Belgium and Italy, the Empire has been a scene of quieter elegances. Whether it was leased to Mr. Gilbert Miller or Miss Cornell, its audiences have invariably represented Sutton Place and the Plaza. One was inclined to reach for a white tie or a string of real pearls when dressing. There was a little band in the balcony above the lobby during the intermissions, a feature which in itself distinguished it from the less conventional theaters managed by more thrift-conscious producers.

As with some favorite aunt, New Yorkers have been forever remembering anniversaries and sentimental occasions on which to do the Empire proud. Its twenty-fifth and fortieth birthdays were suitably marked, but by long odds the stateliest barn-raising was imagined for its half-century mark not so long ago, when all kinds of souvenirs were trotted out, and Walter Hampden, as president of the Players, read from the stage an editorial from the columns of the *Herald Tribune* which had been the product of the same spavined Royal as is typing the copy of this book.

The beautiful Miss Katharine Brush, whom the

writer had squired for the occasion in a horsecab procured from the Somerset Stables, was apprehensive lest,
carried away with the incense of flattery he should rise
to his feet and take an unsolicited bow.

"Sit tight, you dope, and remember your editorial
anonymity," she hissed fit to be heard as far as the
ladies' powdering room.

Another momentous occasion was upon the achievement of its thousandth performance of *Life with
Father,* which was by that time showering an embar-
rassment of riches upon its proprietors: these included
Russel Crouse and Howard Lindsay, Frank Sullivan,
Howard Cullman, and other notables whose income
taxes were too large as they stood. To mark this epic
occasion, Dick Maney, doyen of Broadway press agents,
was called into conference and conceived the notion of
giving a free party for practically all Times Square.
Sherry (the same Louis Sherry, of course, who figured
in the script of *Father*) was induced to erect and shore
up a hundred-foot bar in the lobby, and all the thirsty
of Longacre Square were solicited to attend.

There was no counting the house that night, but it
took a detail of twenty uniformed policemen from the
Fourteenth Precinct Station to protect the waiters, and
the amount, including Sherry's bill for shattered crystal
and purloined napery, when the auditors came the next
day to charge it all off to "Promotion and Publicity,"
was gratifying beyond the wildest expectations of all
concerned.

4

GUIDE AND ESCORT

IT wasn't so very long ago that the constituted authorities stepped in to put a halt to the activities of a young man of bad complexion and considerable enterprise who had evolved what he chose to call a "guide and escort service," but which the police claimed was more in the nature of a service supplying personable young men in fancy attire at the convenience and disposal of solvent females too elderly or lacking in enthusiasm for the chase to go out and procure their own.

The guide and escort service, as a flourishing employment agency for male juveniles, has ceased to exist, but the function it served neither came into being with its rise nor disappeared with its decline, and there are thousands and thousands of New Yorkers who devote large portions of their time, resources, and energy to being guides and escorts. Some of them are bankers and industrialists of impressive proportions; others are less important folk in the eyes of the world, but all are professional New Yorkers and all of them embark on

a career filled with terrors and confusions by the mere
virtue of having permanent residence somewhere within
commuting distance of Broadway and the precincts of
Park Avenue.

It is one of the major hazards of being a New Yorker,
as well as one of his greatest sources of pride, especially
among newspapermen or professional folk who are supposed to know everybody and have the inside track on
everything, that he can take on the out-of-towner who
wants to be shown the works. Nothing so delights the
Gothamite as to point-with-pride, especially among the
saloons and hot spots, and, paradoxically, nothing
frightens him so much as the menace of the visiting
pompier who descends on the town, filled with health,
funds, and enthusiasm and the very worst of intentions
for his annual running amuck with the butlered bon
ton and savoring the touted carnalities of the latter-
day Babylon. For the past fifty-one weeks the pilgrim
to the bazaars and bagnios has been dreaming up perfectly hellish schemes of razzle-dazzle and yippee, and
he doesn't intend to see a bed for any purpose whatsoever while he's in Manhattan. No siree. Laughing and
playing games and occasionally setting fire to the premises and shooting a waiter captain are all he wants. The
very notion of going home before eight in the morning
is humorous to him, and his capacity for strong waters
and kicking in doors along Fifty-second Street is at once
wonderful and terrible. He's read about all the new
places, and the evening that he doesn't take in the Stork,
Morocco, Monte Carlo, the Diamond Horseshoe, Blue
Angel, the Astor Bar, Bill Dwyer's Sawdust Trail, La
Conga, Reuben's, and Leon and Eddie's is an evening

wasted. It's not the expense that sorrows the hospitable urbanite, even though a night on the town for two will run to $150 or better, or even the curious misinformation to the effect that "Oh, you newspaper men get everything free"; it's the idea that "You New Yorkers live this way all the time" that frets his being. If he lived this way all the time his address would be Woodlawn Cemetery.

As remarked above, persons living west of the Hudson nowadays are apt to know a darnsite more about what goes on in Manhattan than nine-tenths of the strap riders on the Seventh Avenue subway. Only advertising agencies and radio announcers persist in the archaic belief that all references to urban sophistication have to be either modified or explained for the out-of-town subscribers. The fact of the matter is that the supposedly naïve and pop-eyed provincials get a hearty horse laugh out of advertising copy geared to the yokel mind and wearily turn off the radio program which attempts to interpret New York in terms of six-year-old bucolic intelligence. Every literate citizen in Emporia, Kansas, knows to the last gusset what Valentina Schlee wore night before last at the benefit performance of *Oklahoma!* and is familiar with every detail of the latest scandal involving Jean Malin's widow or Paul Flato or what emaciated and apparently undernourished beauty George Jean Nathan is squiring at the moment. Soda poppers in Houston and filling-station attendants in the last water-stop town on the Missouri Pacific, which is Prosser, Nebraska, can tell you whether Clare Boothe Brokaw Luce serves a Bollinger Brut or an English cuvée Clicquot at her dinner parties and who is young

Bobby Glaenzer's candy lamb of the moment, as of lunchtime day before yesterday at Voisin's.

Manhattan is no longer a town shrouded in wonder and druidic mystery so far as the rest of the United States is concerned. The contents of the menu of the Ritz are more familiar to millions than the bill of fare

"You New Yorkers live this way all the time!"

at the local depot restaurant, for the simple enough reason that New York is the most written-about, publicized, and exploited urban midst that has ever captured a national imagination. The least detail of its glitter life is a household commonplace from Seattle to Tallahassee, and the person who imagines that New

York exists for New Yorkers alone is making a goat of himself from the word go. The truth is nobody knows the town quite so thoroughly as the ribbon-counter girl in Little Rock, Arkansas, who reads every syndicated column, every coated-paper smart periodical, and every stick of copy about Babylon-on-the-Hudson on which she can lay hands. Compared to her any Manhattanite who tries to set himself up as the town crier is a rube of fantastic proportions.

Having been apprised of these dazzlements of urban existence through the agency of scores of syndicated paragraphers, fashion writers, lady interviewers, glamour whoopers, and radio broadcasters, no one of whom has ever been known to spare a superlative or muff a chance to paint the lily, suburbia wants to see the great original in full blast. The visiting fireman is disappointed if a given evening doesn't provide him with the spectacle of at least one important attempt at mayhem at the Stork Club, of Richard Knight dancing on his hands in the street, and of the dowager Mrs. Vanderbilt taking a chunk out of a society columnist with her bare teeth at a ringside table at Versailles. There's no explaining that these are rare and isolated diversions from the normal, gala moments in the lives of even the most case-hardened New Yorkers themselves. The dinner-coated *gobemouche* from Cleveland knows different! Such things happen all the time, and he reads about them in Louis Sobol!

And your resident New Yorker, trapped by his own expansive chronicles of life among the palefaces when he has been on tour in Kansas City or North Platte, and obligated to return the hospitality of his hosts in

Seattle or Santa Barbara, is in merest duty-bound to provide excitements for his guests even if the effort lands him, the day after their departure for home, in the hospital and the hands of the Morris Plan. For this reason he speeds his friends aboard the Spirit of St. Louis or the Lake Shore Limited, contented of heart and cirrhosed of liver, smelling of arnica from falling in trash cans, their baggage clattering with souvenirs filched from the Club 18 and the Persian Room, with the assurance that "this is the way we live in New York all the time; it's just a little segment out of our regular life." And he's telling the truth.

5

CLOSE THAT TRANSOM!

AMERICANS of the more opulent traveling set have never entirely recovered from the hotel-bedroom existence which came into being as a social by-product of prohibition, and vestigial traces of the room-service civilization will probably be discernible to social archæologists generations from now. During the years of the great foolishness, when the practice of every sort of social courtesy and foregathering was forced from public resorts and survived only behind the doors of suites in a thousand Ritzes, Statlers, and Bellevue-Plazas, there came into being a depraved but amiable taste for conducting all pleasure jaunts in hotel bedrooms, even though the scene might be in some foreign land immune to the great American lunacy. People went to Europe and spent entire summers howling and hurrahing in apartments at the Savoy, the Adlon, or the nearest Hotel of France and the Universe, without so much as poking a nose outdoors except for occasional safaris on the night-

Brothers in a fellowship of lost causes

club districts. At home they went to New London for
the Yale and Harvard boat races in June but never got
nearer the Thames than the third floor of the Griswold
over the entire week-end. They saw none of the Santa
Barbara fiesta because they were locked up in a cottage
at the Biltmore or in Nick Ludington's beach house.

At Saratoga they followed the races from a drawing-
room suite in the United States Hotel, and happy revelers on the way to the Bohemian Grove have been known
to become trapped upstairs in the San Francisco Fairmont and miss everything. The hotel bedroom party
givers became a sort of Cole Porter group of international celebrities whose password was "Room Service"

and who seldom saw daylight save en route to another
city and another hotel.

Even in a land redeemed and of a happier time they
still will survive here and there. The author recently encountered a group of impious acquaintances in a parlor
suite in the Texas Hotel at Fort Worth. They were
commanding orange ice by the quart at one o'clock in
the morning to be shaken up with an equal quantity
of mother's ruin, despite the fact that Texans incline to
frown upon observance of their own liquor statutes and
that several cafés were dispensing fun potage within the
block. We knew then that we were in the presence of
unreconstructed spirits stemming from the legendary
past, brothers-in-arms of the Jacobins, companions of
the Confederacy, bathrobe and pajama-bottom brothers
in the fellowship of all the world's lost causes, and committed forever to drinking to the King Over the Ice
Water in the hotel pitcher which the boy brings up
the hall.

6

GUSTATORY SOUVENIRS

THE cold boiled pompano with a mustard cream sauce, first encountered many years ago at the Patio Lamaze in Palm Beach and a remembered wonder and glory ever since.

The deviled grilled beef bones which once used to be and, for the matter of that, still may be featured at Durgin and Parks' market man's restaurant opposite Faneuil Hall Market in Boston.

The most satisfying and restorative clam juice cocktails in the world compounded from a secret formula (mostly hot stuffs) and shaken in a cocktail mixer by Gi-Gi at the Coq Rouge.

The roulade of sand dabs at the Palace in San Francisco and the incredible petit cœur à la crême aux fraises rafraichies at the same place.

The jugged saddle of hare at Luchow's, a miracle of fine lean meat that requires weeks of stewing and sousing in red wine as preparation.

The moules marinières, top-ranking dish of the celebrated menu at the Lafayette, not to mention their

43

baby guinea fowl en casserole, "in the manner of grand-mother," as the French has it.

The baked lobster Savannah at Locke-Ober's Winter Place Wine Rooms in Boston, rushed practically smoldering from the kitchens by old Nick Stuhl, the patron, himself.

The rack of lamb served his guests by Fred Wildman at Bellows & Co.'s private dining room at their shop in Fifty-second Street, flanked by bottles of Brane-Cantenac 1900 and followed by green salad and real Brie cheese.

The thick, creamy chicken soup at the Plaza, a miraculous Sunday restorative if accompanied by a couple of Mike's driest Martinis.

The shrimp Creole served, of all places, aboard the Illinois Central's Panama Limited en route between Chicago and New Orleans and as good as anything available in the Creole culinary capital itself.

The minute steaks which the Park Lane runs up for late customers at Tuesday Dutch Treat lunches if the regular entrée has run out, a handsome premium on tardiness.

The tenderloin steak sandwiches at Jack Bleeck's Artists and Writers, the best money's worth of wonderful cow anywhere in Manhattan.

The real, genuine, authentic, veritable Strasbourg foie gras which, until recently was—and may still be—available to old friends of the house at Chateaubriand in East Fifty-sixth Street.

The sidecars—sneer if you will, you purists and gastronomic snoots—at Perino's in Wilshire in Los Angeles.

Folk have been known to travel thousands of miles for them.

The cheeses of Crowley of Vermont, the factual refutation of the legend that Yankees are barbarians at table.

The heavenly hamburgers at Hamburger Heaven in Madison Avenue. Beware of the gyp-burgers and bogus-burgers of envious imitators. Only the original will do.

The Moet and Chandon's '21 bottling of Dom Perignon champagne, a few flasks of which are still available at the Pump Room in Chicago. Also any of the deviled dishes, house specialties at Ernie Byfield's, most elaborate of all mid-continental restaurants.

The pâté maison at the very nice Baroque in Fifty-third Street, not to mention the pompano belle meunière, the venison steak grand veneur, and almost everything on the menu, for the matter of that.

The stingers, specially compounded according to the formula of Radio Technician C. M. Clegg, U. S. N. R. (almost all Hennessy and practically no mint at all) by Gus Boell at the men's bar in the St. Francis, San Francisco.

The softshell crabs, when the season is on, an immemorial New York institution over at Gage and Tollner's in Brooklyn, where it has been since the Year One.

The omelets of all sorts confected in New York's smallest restaurant, Maison Louis de Lyon, in East Fifty-sixth Street, which seats only ten customers and serves nothing but omelets and the trimmings.

The Delaware shad roe bonne femme, at the St. Regis, first and most welcome of all the harbingers of spring.

The escalopini of veal at the Colony Restaurant, a specialty and favorite of Gene Cavallero, who learned a trick or two in his native Italy.

The so-called Sierra cheese which comes aboard the Santa Fé trains for the fortunate as they near California, the whole supply being the property of the railroad.

The terrapin stew on the menu at Harvey's ancient restaurant in the Federal City—a miracle if you have the patience to wait upon the whims and convenience of the colored servitors.

The Hines Triomphe, available elsewhere, but still seeming like the cleanest and finest liqueur Cognac in the world on the premises of its importers, Jack and Charlie's "21."

The eggs gashouse at the New York Yacht Club, another of those chef's secrets but, generally speaking, an elegant arrangement of baked eggs en casserole atop a skilfully compounded cheese fondue.

On Saturday nights in New England the kidney beans baked by Friend's Bakery in Malden, Massachusetts, but generally available throughout the region and something divorced from all the other baked beans in the world.

The creamed chipped beef which this writer is accustomed to absorb daily for breakfast at the Madison and which carries him through a morning of writing copy like this.

The breakfast steaks, a good full pound of T-bone flanked with approximately a peck of home-fried potatoes aboard the streamliner City of San Francisco.

The crabs Moro à la mode de Havana, at Antoine's in New Orleans, not forgetting that old culinary cliché, the oysters Rockefeller. Nobody's ever been able to say they were less than superlative.

The Scotch grouse rôti nature and the pheasant en casserole with cabbage and whole carrots at that shrine of Manhattan gastronomy, Jack and Charlie's.

The Manhattan cocktails at Mulligan and Rourke's Saloon (otherwise known as the Biltmore Hotel) in New York, built with a specially doctored whisky and about the best in the land.

The English mutton chops at Frankie and Johnnie's at Forty-fifth and Eighth, served in a midst whose uproar suggests nothing so much as feeding hour at the North Brothers' Circus.

7

BOOM TOWN DE LUXE

THERE has long been established a legend to the effect that good Americans when they die go, not to heaven, but to Paris. Time has changed all that, but, even before events made such transatlantic emigration improbable, there lurked in many minds a suspicion that better Americans, when they died, went to San Francisco, and that the very best people of all went to San Francisco while they were still alive. Certainly there are thousands of discerning Yankees who wouldn't trade a cycle of the dusty and over-touted wonderments of a spavined European capital for a week-end in the plaisances of the world's most beautiful city in the shadow of the Oakland Bridge. Paris never had a frontier legend or an only yesterday peopled with the Comstock kings, the vigilantes, the railroad builders and the Faro-bank gamblers of Kearny Street. It never had the Palace or stingers in the Happy Valley Bar or the moon over Nob Hill or the cable-cars or parades in Market Street; and the author, for one, wouldn't trade the Bay of Naples for the least cesspool

of the Mission District or the architecture of Notre
Dame for the plush and ormolu glory of the Fairmont
lobby.

A city of fabulous past and glittering present, city of
bonanza times and fires, city of railroads and gold and
banks and ships and luxury hotels, city of a hundred
banners rippling from skyscraper roofs, city of vigilantes and Pisco punches, city of incredible hills and
mists and vistas, city of the most spacious and gusty
saga in the American story, a sailor city, a rich man's
city, a city of glamour and ghosts of the Barbary Coast,
San Francisco recapitulates to-day almost every phase
of its fragrant past and is the super de luxe boom town
of a wartime nation.

The original overlords of the Central Pacific Railroad,
the political pirates and plunderers of the nineteenth
century, the celebrated cocktail route, the mansions of
the great nabobs on the hilltops, the wickedness of
Chinatown and the Barbary Coast, much that was tangible and animate in the San Francisco story may be
gone, but the hilarious mortmain of the past is discernible even to gobs in the stews of Market Street
who never heard of Crocker or Sutro or the Poodle Dog
or the Mizners or a Palace whose inner court was the
carriage drive. Through lean years, disastrous strikes,
labor agitation and bankruptcies, the San Francisco
wheel has come full circle. The town is in the chips, the
fleet is always in; the plush cord is up in the hot spots
and you can't fight your way to the bar at cocktail time
at the Top of the Mark, the Fairmont, or Timmy
Fleuger's ornate version of a gin parlor at the St. Francis.
Luncheon again is a great and stately function at the

Palace; Slapsy Maxy Rosenbloom has an upstairs *el dumpo* which makes his Hollywood den look like something out of Watteau.

Even in the leanest years of the shipping and hotel strike, San Francisco never completely lost its flavor or identity; now it is reëstablished, not perhaps to the Bohemian tastes of such notables as Major J. Edward Bowes or the late Arnold Genthe, but certainly in terms of a luxuriousness and panache of excitement which makes it, along with Boston, Charleston, and New Orleans and New York, a characteristic and individual community.

Nowhere else are there such immemorial institutions as cable-cars, Sunday expeditions to the Cliff House to see the seals, the view from the Top of the Mark and from Julius' Castle, the tumults of what apparently are a million sailors in the Market Street stewing, spewing and tattooing parlors after dark, the fabled sweep of the Bay Bridge, the stingers built by Gus, the ageless barkeep at the St. Francis men's buffet, the tiny shrimp, sand dabs and giant crabs' legs that make the town a mecca for gourmets, the urgency of conflagrations in a community acutely fire conscious, the sibilant sub-pavement whisper of endless cables for the cable-cars, the ceaseless pageant of arrival and departure for wars and the far places of the earth. Other communities may have their counterparts and parallel fascinations, but in their entirety, these are the property of San Francisco alone.

Perhaps the most perfumed of all San Francisco legends and one that has survived from the age of the railroad kings and the Comstock Lode, the Palace (perish the thought of calling it the Palace "Hotel") still stands in its post-conflagration redaction, a mighty souvenir of the champagne past and the bonanza present. An older Palace had been, in the days of Huntington, Crocker, Mackay, and Flood, virtually the seat of the government of California. Legend surrounds its every mention, and books by the bookshelf yard have been written about it. Leland Stanford was the first guest to register at the old Palace; Charles Crocker was the first to enter its dining-room. King Kalakaua had died there as Warren G. Harding was to die in a later Palace. Grant and Sherman, Adelina Patti, McKinley and Henry Ward Beecher were familiars to its corridors. Frank Norris and Ambrose Bierce and the elder and younger Hearsts knew it well. Its free lunch of game birds and foie gras was fabled, and it was a more than train-orders stop on the cocktail route of the nineties.

To-day, the Palace is the strongest connecting link between the San Francisco of spacious times during the last century and the epic San Francisco of the present. Its food is tops for the Pacific Coast, its kitchens reputedly the best organized anywhere west of the Waldorf; the cocktail hour under Maxfield Parrish's Pied Piper, a dubious triumph of art but a landmark of note, necessitates the passing of over-shoulder drinks by the bucket brigade system from the bar to thirsty brokers and admirals in the rear. Midweek lunch in its Palm Court, once the carriage entrance to the premises, is institutional and immutable, the counterpart of Monday lunch in the Mural Room at the St. Francis. Its menu teems with dishes of the Palace tradition: Consommé Patti, created many years ago by Chef Ernest Arbogast in honor of the singer, roulade of sand dabs, foie gras and marrow broiled on toast, petit cœur flottant à la crême aux fraises. The transition from champagne days to the age of sidecars the Palace has taken in its stride. Its several restaurants are jammed at mealtimes (it set an all-time record recently by serving luncheon for 4,200 persons in a single day, and in the men's bar, the Happy Valley and adjacent sluicing premises, the business of hoisting them is nearly a twenty-four-hour procedure. Its tremendous corridors and public rooms are celebrated for the flowers and, indeed, whole shrubs and trees brought to town daily from the hotel's own greenhouses at South San Francisco.

The men's bar of the Palace at lunch is a fine thing to behold, peopled as it is with the mighty and witty of the town: Paul Posz of the Municipal Opera; Timothy Fleuger, the ribald architect who has just finished installing a four-story subcellar garage under Union Chester Rowell, Clarence Lindner, publisher of the San Francisco County; George Cameron of the *Chronicle;* Joe Cauthorn, publisher of the local Scripps-Howard *News;* Joseph Dyer, Jr., the Municipal Art Commissioner; sometimes Mayor Rossi, and invariably a platoon or two of ensigns and junior loueys from the Navy and, on week-ends, shoals of enlisted men from the training school at Treasure Island. A feature of lunch at the Palace is the "Cabinet Table" in the Palm Court, regularly seating such notables as John Francis Neylan, Chester Rowell, Clarence Lindner, publisher of the San Francisco *Examiner,* Justices Douglas Edmonds and John Shenk, and Chief Justice Phil Gibson.

Practically coeval with the Palace is the Fairmont

Hotel on the impressive top of Nob Hill, flanked on one façade by the Mark Hopkins and facing the Pacific Union Club whose stately premises were once the Flood mansion. The Fairmont was built by Senator Fair out of the profits from the Comstock in 1903, and was scheduled to open, with vast civic and social ceremony, in June, 1906. In April of that year, however, San Francisco suffered the most epic of its many conflagrations, and along with everything else on Nob Hill, the Fairmont went up in a cloud of the most expensive smoke. The basic architecture of the premises survived, and it opened its doors a year later to become one of the classic hotels de luxe of our continent.

The Fairmont is nothing to trifle with. Its approach is guarded by carriage starters in crimson tail-coats and white plug hats; its corridors are the cloistered equivalent of the landing ramps of a military airfield; its marble pillars, gilded colonnades, Chinoiseries and ornate furniture are the archetypal symbols of solid affluence and respectability. The Cirque Room is, perhaps, the most agreeably conservative hoisting parlor in town, and the senior barkeep, Jack Walker, is reputed to make the most energetic cocktails, bar none, on Nob Hill. The clientele is varied and stretches between Barbara Hutton and Cary Grant and the more affluent gentlemen gobs of the Navy and Coast Guard. An aspect of San Francisco public life which is less familiar in other cities is the almost complete dominance of the better and more costly resorts by enlisted men of the various services and the something less than awe which attends the persons of commissioned officers. No amount of gold braid, oak leaves, and spread eagles can impress a San Francisco waiter captain; seamen and Army privates in general have a sort of social priority almost everywhere. It is a common and heartening sight to see apprentice seamen, pharmacist's mates, and torpedomen bowed to their tables while recent ensigns and self-important majors and their wives wait outside the crimson cord for inferior service and slightly watered drinks. In almost all the bars of the town, the custom obtains of slipping free hookers, dividends, and over-size portions at reduced rates to enlisted men. San Francisco has always been a sailor's town, and another war doesn't change it any.

In a more leisured generation, the cocktail route in San Francisco was a world-famed institution and embraced in its economy all the bars of downtown Montgomery, Market, and Kearny Streets and scores of adjacent premises in stews, mews, and alleyways. According to Evelyn Wells in her *Champagne Days of San Francisco,* the cocktail route started from the Reception Saloon in Sutter Street and terminated in any of a number of celebrated oases in upper Market. High spots in the accepted course of progress were Pop Sullivan's Hoffman Café, the Palace, Haquette's Palace of Art on Post near Kearny, the Occidental in Montgomery, the Bank Exchange with its marble floors and fine paintings, the Baldwin, the Peerless, and the Grand Hotel, Dunne Brothers, Flood and O'Brien's, celebrated for its corned beef and cabbage, and the Cobweb Palace.

The cocktail route still exists in the San Francisco of the moment, but only the Palace survives in the full glory of the Nineties. Unlike New Yorkers, San Franciscans admire to stroll from saloon to saloon, absorb-

Enlisted personnel has priority

ing no more than six or eight liquid arrangements in
each and visiting their favorite haunts with more or
less clock-like regularity. New Yorkers, of course, prefer
to sit themselves down in one haunt and stay sat. Notable among the refuges of contemporary times are the
two bars at the St. Francis, the men's buffet presided
over by Gus Boell, and the shiny patent leather and
composition glass devising of architect Timmy Fleuger
known to irreverent patrons as the "coffin bar," the Top
of the Mark at the Mark Hopkins, the Cirque Room
at the Fairmont across the way, the Prado in the Plaza
Hotel in Union Square, Ray Barrow's, 41 Powell Street,
the Clift Hotel's Redwood Bar, and the Persian Room
at the Sir Francis Drake.

The gaudy night life for which San Francisco has
been notable ever since Mr. Sutter discovered gold up
the Sacramento River continues unabated in its modern recrudescence, financed largely by the military and
the Navy and flowering handsomely from the precincts
of Market Street to the "Beach" and the loud but essentially innocent resorts of the International Settlement.
Mostly the dives of this particular district are rigorously
policed by the municipality and shore and Army gen-
darmes; their viciousness is confined to beer drinking,
shooting at targets, singing Victorian ballads at Bill's
Gay Nineties and being photographed in prop hats by
tintype cameramen who never heard of Arnold Genthe.
There are more oblique amusements for the ultra-sophis-
ticated, but they are well screened from the public gaze,
and the clammy hand of authority clamps a padlock on
them now and then. Fun, generally speaking, is robust,
naïve, and very costly.

Nick at the Palace men's bar can charge $2.50 for a couple of mixed drinks without batting an eye, but he has been known to be generous with enlisted men and is one of the town's highly esteemed citizens. Two bits for a shine is the standard price, and motor livery is expensive beyond the imaginings of anybody who is not a Spreckels or a Crocker. Food, however, is moderately priced even in the poshest places, and dinner at Omar Khayyam's, the Mark, or Maiden Lane Solari's comes to no more than in similar establishments elsewhere in the world.

Omar Khayyam's is a restaurant deserving of more than passing notice, not so much for its food as for the personality of its presiding chef and genius, George Mardikian, who has accomplished for himself and his house one of the more startling jobs of promotion and exploitation of the American restaurant world. So vast has been the success of the establishment that it is practically impossible to secure a table without reservations, and long ranks of the patient wait night after night on the staircase for places.

The show place of Nob Hill is, of course, the Top of the Mark, a tavern of Mr. Fleuger's designing, wonderfully located on the roof of the Mark Hopkins Hotel. Two elevators are required to hoist its patrons skyward, while a single lift is sufficient for the other requirements of the house, and the view from its panoramic windows is breath-taking. The circular bar is jammed three deep with the armed services after sundown, while older officers and their ladies prefer window tables overlooking the harbor or Mission District or the "Beach."

Further exploration of the white light scene would

lead the pious pilgrim to the Bal Tabarin, to the Fiesta, where the Tropical Punch is all that its name implies in the way of a torrid sock, a snack at Julius' Castle, to Slapsy Maxy's in O'Farrell, Mori's, Jack's, John's Rendezvous, the Copacabana, and the Club 400. No survey, however cursory, of the Golden Gate scene would be complete without mention of two restaurants, more or less out of San Francisco's city center: the Cliff House, overlooking the Pacific beyond the Sutro Baths, and Trader Vic's across the bridge in Oakland. There have been numerous versions of the Cliff House, two of them having been destroyed by fire and one by a mysterious internal explosion. It still retains much of its glamour as a week-end roadhouse, when the weather is fair. Vic's trading-post, saloon, and restaurant in Oakland boasts ninety varieties of tall rum drinks alone on its incredible bill of potations, while other goods in trade available are all sorts of souvenirs of the Pacific islands and ships' stores. Vic himself, a ribald fellow who wears a camellia over one ear, is something right out of Conrad.

A city that takes its arts seriously, San Francisco is able to boast that its recent opera season was the most successful in its history, despite wartime conditions. Its handsome and stately Municipal Opera House, under the general administration of Gaetano Merola, is sold out nightly, carrying on a tradition of the city that stems from the gold-rush days of '49.

An older San Francisco heard its opera at Morosco's Grand Opera House on Mission near Third, where, according to tradition, every night when opera wasn't being sung, Walter Morosco would sit in the last row,

weeping copiously over the florid griefs of his own pro-
ductions of *Bertha, the Sewing Machine Girl* and *The
Prodigal Daughter*. According to Miss Wells' chronicle of the time, it was customary for the police to guard
the stage entry after such performances, as the citizenry,
hypnotized by melodramatic villainy, often assembled to
shower the leading heavy with cobblestones. In those
days, Melba, Fritzi Scheff, Nordica, Édouard de Reszke,
Homer, Scotti, Emma Eames, Sembrich, and Caruso
were the city's favorites.

To-day, the Municipal Opera is populated by Lily
Pons, Jean Tennyson, Jan Peerce, Richard Bonelli,
Ezio Pinza, John Brownlee, and Josephine Antoine;
the town and the military turn out in clusters of diamonds and horse blankets of sables every bit as impressive as the Metropolitan on a more Cartier–Revillon
Frères evening. As a matter of fact the architectural
economy of the Memorial Opera lends itself far more
than the Met to spectacular parading, with its broad
staircases, endless marble gangways, and vast white-and-
gold lobby. There are bars for every one, one of them
devoted to champagne exclusively, and every one from
Dorothy Spreckels Dupuy McCarthy to Mme. Margaret
Chung, the energetic and public-spirited over-lady of
Chinatown, can be seen parading at the intermissions
of *The Bartered Bride, Fledermaus,* or *Masked Ball*.
Later in the season, the Municipal bill includes a stand
by the Russian Ballet Theater and a concert calendar
embracing Stokowski, Marian Anderson, Risë Stevens,
the Don Cossacks, Richard Crooks, Jascha Heifetz,
Mischa Elman, John Charles Thomas, Nelson Eddy,
and Artur Rubinstein.

To argue that the San Francisco scene is the archetype of luxurious perfection would be as erroneous as such an unqualified estimate would be of any boom town. It suffers many of the inconveniences of being a bonanza town and at the same time a community hedged, hindered, and harassed by the circumstance of war. Hotel space is at a fabulous premium, and weary and unsuccessful searchers for accommodations snooze gently throughout the night unmolested in the lobbies of the smartest caravanserais. Always short of transportation, it is a city where twenty times the number of taxis now in service wouldn't begin to fill the demand, and a hack once captured is usually retained by the lucky finder at meter rates no matter how long his stops may be. Competent waiters are almost non-extant, and elderly captains serve in a variety of capacities ranging from wine steward to bus. There is an almost unbelievable shortage of imported wine in a town once famed for its cellars. All the irregularities and nuisances incidental to Federal control of everything are manifest and abundant, but San Francisco rises above them and probably will continue to do so for the duration. Once termed a town "where hospitality is a vice," public entertaining in restaurants and night clubs is practically unabated, even though the hostess may have to rush drinks from the bar herself.

Boom town and bonanza, San Francisco retains so much of the feeling and spirit of its other palmy days, when "seeing the elephant" was a favorite local phrase for doing the rounds of the more elaborate joy-boy bars, schnitzel châteaux, bagnios, and deadfalls, that Senator William Sharon or Jack London or any other old-timer,

In Post Street, gunfire; in Market, the can-can

if he were to return to earth blindfolded, would still recognize the city from its immemorial street sounds alone. The thunder of the four tracks of street-cars in Market, the incessant uproar of fire companies en route to conflagration or false alarm, the clang of the cable-car bells, distinctive and unique in all the world, the fog-horns in the harbor on misty nights, the roars of ship-bound sailors heading vaguely for the Ferry House at dawn, the bedlamite cries of news vendors with the morning editions out at seven the previous evening, the chimes of the churches, all have about them the wistful and ageless quality of America's most exciting city. If ever they should be stilled, something of the wonder of the nation's life of gusto and hurrah would be gone forever.

8

WHO'S IN WHAT SALOON NOW?

THE phenomenon of American society, it is almost a
cliché to remark, has always provided for the
impious-minded observer the best features of
Hallowe'en at the madhouse and Ringling Brothers' Barnum and Bailey Circus at its most gaudy
pitch of hurrah in the days of the consulship over
its destinies of John and Buddy North. Since the first
pair of substantial pewter nose stilts were purchased by
an early Dutch madam in Maiden Lane the day after she
emerged from a lower Manhattan house of mirth to
marry a wealthy sea captain with genuine silver buckles
on his shoes, the nose-stilt industry, along with the in-
terlocking directorates of the tiara bazaars, lorgnette
foundries, and coat-armor forgers, has paid enormous
dividends and is allowed as gilt edge investment, even
for trust funds, in most states.

The manifestations of patrician circumstance have
varied naturally enough with the seasons and the place.
In the earlier colonies there was an association with
landed property and feudal obligations. After the

American Revolution its hallmarks became rum and
niggers in the North Atlantic States and whisky and
niggers in the South. After the Civil War and to this
day it is possible to identify a true southern aristocrat
by his professional poverty and dexterity in bad manners and the northern nabob by a faint aroma of William James and the Grand Tour. The real boom, of
course, which brought on the finest excitements and
biggest bathtubs in society derived from the bonanzas
and golcondas of the wonderful West.

To the author, the quintessential great lady of American society has always been the Unsinkable Mrs. Brown
of Denver, but she merits and, indeed, has received
the attention of greater scholars and observers of the
human comedy, and there is no room for the emblazon-
ing here of the immortal saga of her progress through
the palaces of two continents. Only Gene Fowler can
do it.

During the thirties of the twentieth century, as a consequence of a number of causes and occasions touched
upon later, New York society, which has always set the
national *ton* of de luxe living, despite agitated head-
tossings and anguished cries of "Me, I'm the prettiest"
from Boston, Philadelphia, Washington, Charleston,
and other suburban points, found itself living frankly,
unabashedly, and almost entirely in saloons.

It wasn't any very startling revolution, but the exploitation to which the night-club era was exposed, more
than anything else through the agency of intimate photography of celebrities in the tonier taprooms, soon
caused it to become known as café society, and the rise
and flowering of this particular generation of a café

society that had always been in existence was the occasion of a vast deal of publicity, pother, and, of course, profit to all concerned.

Even the origin of the phrase itself enlisted the attentions of research experts, and the late Maury Paul (Cholly Knickerbocker of the Hearst papers), the last of the truly competent society reporters, every time the words café society were used by any one else in print, emitted banshee screeches and jumped up and down on his hat in the Colony Restaurant to call attention to the circumstance that he had originated it and it was his property. Nobody ever attempted to dispute his claim of authorship—nobody in his right mind would ever run foul of Maury in any matter—but the phrase became pretty common currency, and the matter of its copyright was never seriously in dispute.

The balance of this chapter depicts the closing years of the thirties, while the lights of the world were still dazzlingly ablaze, and is recalled from the oblivion of the files as a nosegay, a period picture, as dated and archaic as grandfather with his hand thrust into the folds of his Prince Albert. The period in Manhattan's tinsel progress through the years is as clearly defined and as easily distinguishable for its own characteristics as the times of Philip Hone or the Florida Water age of Ward McAllister or the years of the great tea dance of Scott Fitzgerald, and it is left in the spirit in which it was written to emphasize its part in a period pattern. Almost every one of the physical premises in which its characters have their setting are to-day flourishing as the haunts of another generation of café society, but the spirit of the age that produced it is something for the attention of the historians and the champions of lost causes.

The swarthy carriage starter in the blue uniform of the Foreign Legion, complete with kepi and pugree, saluted you with a *"Bon soir, m'sieu, madame,"* as the line of limousines' shiny bonnets edged up to the marquee on the south side of East Fifty-fourth Street. He was Senegalese and spoke no English, but there were two other liveried doormen and as many uniformed police officers on duty who were adequate in both speech and action, should either be required. There was never any trouble at El Morocco, perhaps New York's costliest and most representative night club, and in the thirties, it was generally acknowledged, the world's most opulent parade ground for the celebrities of fashionable "café society."

Inside the door there were several hard-faced gentlemen in dinner clothes and two or three coat-check girls of positively iridescent beauty. And beyond them was Carino, most urbane of waiter captains and a diplomat on whose favors and discretion hung feuds and romances, careers, aspirations, and the very foundations of the most bitterly jealous and competitive social hierarchy of our generation. Fortunes and professional careers were made by sitting at the right table at Morocco, believe it or not, and people were known to leave town because Carino had said he was sorry, but all the tables were reserved that evening.

The tangible décor of El Morocco might not have impressed you. Neither would the floor show, for the reason that there wasn't any. It was a long, low room —once a store—decorated in deep blue and white, with palm trees of gold leaf along the walls and tiny stars winking on and off in the azure ceiling. There was a modest-sized dance floor and at one end a stand-up bar presided over by half a dozen expert youths in spotless white. There were many more spectacular night clubs in New York, but El Morocco seemed at the time *the* night club—that is why it is being described here at length—and when you looked at the people who were patronizing it, you at once knew why.

Naturally, El Morocco was not the one and only night club in Manhattan to which the élite of the social and professional front repaired for midnight-to-breakfast merriment and parade. It was unique in that it offered no show or entertainment, but there were half a dozen other night clubs and hotel restaurants where the carriage trade flashed their lorgnons over the bird and cold bottle of tradition after the theater: the infinitely smart Persian Room at the conservative Plaza Hotel; Sherman Billingsley's Stork Club; the Iridium Room at the St. Regis, or the Rainbow Room on the tip-top floor of the RCA Building at Radio City. Then, too, there had been a revival of the after-theater supper as a serious meal without music or entertainment of any sort, and at the Colony Restaurant, at Theodore's, and at Jack and Charlie's, folk who had dined hastily off a highball before the show might be seen setting to work on Scotch grouse, pheasant en casserole, firkins of Strasbourg foie gras, quail in aspic, vanilla soufflé, and gilt-foiled bottles of heroic proportions.

But somehow, perhaps by some process of sheer emergent evolution, John Perona attracted to his El Morocco the patronage of the most spectacular celebrities of America's café society, and café society was the only society of that day that amounted to a hill of *haricots verts*.

It was a gala night at Morocco, although the difference between a *fête de grand luxe* and an evening of regular business was discernible only to the trained eye of an expert reporter of the urban scene, like Maury Paul or Nancy Randolph. Surging in a flood tide of imperial sables and diamond-and-ruby necklaces, caressed by squalls and cat's paws of costly perfumes, was the most glittering parade of names that made news, of chichi and chinchilla, since the days of Peacock Alley, when the Waldorf was at Thirty-fourth Street and Fifth Avenue.

Morocco was maintained on the basis that the most exciting floor show in the world was provided by the patrons themselves. Two crack orchestras provided continuous music from dinner till dawn. As the evening progressed and the press of patrons became greater, tables were set up on the border of the postage-stamp dance space, further and further infringing upon the parquet until, on a really full night, the entire floor was covered and there was no dancing at all. Folk went there to see and to be seen, to be photographed by Jerome Zerbe, socialite and the first of the "candid cameramen" to invade the privacy of society and to make notes on who was keeping company with whom.

The most opulent furs, wraps insured for fifty and sixty thousand dollars, a wide predominance of white ties over the informal dinner-jacket, emeralds and sapphires so costly that insurance companies kept the premises patrolled at all times by guards in evening dress, the single eye-glasses of titled foreigners, and the appraising glances of a stag line of beautifully manicured youths at the bar were the commonplaces of the house. The café set of Manhattan firmly believed that if a given celebrity failed to show up at Morocco three or four times a week he was dead, or, worse still, out of town.

On the dance floor at one time might be seen such a social mixed grill as Hope Williams, of stage fame, in a short ermine coat and blazing necklace of emeralds, dancing with Whitney Bolton, debonair and dapper managing editor of the *Morning Telegraph* and one of the two New York reporters to sport an imported motorcar; George Djamgaroff, mystery man of the White Russian colony, with the boyishly monocled Edla Frankau, a leading fashion expert; Moss Hart, most successful of musical playwrights, his arm around the shoulder of Tallulah Bankhead; Van Voorhees, voice of the March of Time, with Mrs. Harrison Williams; the adolescent Jimmy Donahue, brother of the better-known Woolworth Donahue, with Babe Palmer of the famous Chicago tribe of Potter Palmers; Herbert Marshall, the screen star.

Archetypal, perhaps, of the ultra-fashionables who had, in a manner, abdicated from "Cave Dweller" society—or the "Four Hundred"— in favor of the gayer activities and more elastic contacts of café society, was Mrs. Williams, often tagged by news writers, "New York's smartest woman." Reported to spend a hundred and fifty thousand dollars a year on her wardrobe alone, Mrs. Williams was far from being a mere mannequin gracefully revolving in a chromium mist of cocktail-party sophistication and the florid gestures of publicized mediocrities.

So sound was her taste in matters of art that she was once taken by a London shopkeeper for a fellow professional as a result of her knowledge of Chinese ceramics. Having parted on the best of terms from two previous husbands, she was the wife of a public-utilities magnate and was as much of an arbiter in social vogues as he was in the world of light and water-power.

The famous "white" drawing-room of her magnificent mansion on Fifth Avenue set a style in white furniture and décor which swayed the taste of every interior decorator in the land, and her four-hundred-foot German-built yacht *Warrior* was the scene of the smartest entertaining of the seasons, as the tide of finance and fashion ebbed and flowed from Long Island to Palm Beach and to Newport.

"Birth," Mrs. Williams once said, "no longer is the prime requisite of society. If there is a society, it has leveled to personalities of intelligence or cleverness or interest, or to those who are just well liked and have enough money to maintain themselves with reasonable conventional comforts. And that is as it should be."

At a table facing the door, which was reserved for the proprietor and his guests, were a group of the ranking society reporters of the town, as beautifully dressed as the paying guests, earning their daily plover's eggs. Without their presence, and that of the dinner-jacketed photographers, no evening at Morocco would have been complete.

An aspect of the social comedy as it was played in the thirties which would have grieved the members of

"Cave Dweller" society of the Murray Hill and gas-
lamp era was the attitude of café society toward the
reports of its activities in the metropolitan press. Social
prestige in 1937 was rated by linage in the papers, and
such society reporters as Maury Paul, Mme. Flutterbye
and Reggie (Baron George Wrangel) of the *Journal,*
or Nancy Randolph of the *Daily News* fulfilled much
the same function at a party as do reviewers at a new
play.

No hostess considered her party a success, no matter
how much pleasure she might have afforded her guests,
unless it received favorable notices in next day's newspapers. Just as there was a Critics' Circle of drama reviewers which included such luminaries as John Mason
Brown, Gilbert Gabriel, Richard Watts, Jr., and Brooks
Atkinson, there might very well have been a Society
Reporters' League of Helen Worden, Barclay Beekman, and George Lowther, 3rd, the last of whom sometimes doubled for George Wrangel. Their functions, in
their special fields, were very similar.

In many cases society reporters were themselves accredited members of the circles in which they moved,
while others were *ex officio* participants in the smarter
routs and revels of the faubourgs. The late Maury Paul,
stoutish, jolly, and an amazingly informed chronicler
of metropolitan doings, was recognized as the leader of
all social scribes. He was a member of a Philadelphia
family whose legend and coat armor went back beyond
the Revolution. Molly Cogswell Thayer (Mme. Flutterbye) was married to a son of the Reverend William
Greenough Thayer, long the venerated head of St.
Mark's School at Southborough, Massachusetts, one of

the two most churchly and aristocratic boys' preparatory schools in the country. Baron Wrangel was a member of the Continental family of that name.

But to return to Morocco—where the stags *pro tem.* lined the bar downing highballs at a dollar a glass or champagne cocktails for one-fifty. Among them on a given evening might be seen Kip Soldwedel, a glittering young man of the boulevards; Jack Velie of Kansas City, a nephew of Dwight Deere Wiman and one of the proprietors of the Deere plow works; Emlen Etting, the Philadelphia modernist painter; Bill Hearst and his young brother, Randy; Delos Chappell, producer who revived the Central City Opera House in Colorado for a week's run of *Camille,* which set him back two hundred and fifty thousand dollars; Winsor French, columnist of the Cleveland *Press,* on a Manhattan jaunt; Bill Okie, display designer for a Fifth Avenue jeweler; "Junior" Wotkyns, a dazzling youth from Hollywood and the heart-throb at that moment of Libby Holman Reynolds; Quentin Reynolds, the fictioneer; Jack Kriendler of "Jack and Charlie" and "Mooey-Mooey" fame; Louis Sobol of the *Journal,* and Nat Saltonstall, most eligible bachelor of Boston, over for the week-end.

Later, the stags would be augmented by Dwight Fiske, who had just finished singing his wickedly satirical ballads over at the Savoy-Plaza; Arthur Cooley, the champagne salesman, with the Marquis de Polignac, his boss; Howard Hughes, the film producer, and Stanley Sackett, the hotel man, said to be the original of Peter Arno's surprised-looking gent with the bald head and waxed mustaches who is always finding himself in such peculiar jams.

The bar was well thronged by two o'clock, but no-body needed to stand there longer than he wished, be-cause every one in the room knew almost every one else, and any personable somebody was asked to sit at some friend's table every other minute.

Let us for a moment, however, desert the mink and monocles of Morocco and glance deeper into the past to see if there is visible there the origin of what the thirties called café society.

It is impossible to date arbitrarily the beginning of an important social trend, but to say that the arrival of Addison and Wilson Mizner on the Manhattan scene marked the start of the evolution of café society is close to being the truth. These rowdy, tumultuous, and gusty brothers from California descended on formal society —what was known as the "Four Hundred." Their fabu-lous adventures and spacious gestures became a national saga.

Before they got through, Wilson had married Mrs. Charles T. Yerkes, who had inherited fifty million dol-lars the month before from her traction-magnate hus-band, and Addison turned out to be the architect who laid out Palm Beach as it is to-day. And the two of them had laughed so hard at formal society that society started laughing at itself.

That was the beginning of the end. Society as it was then constituted laughed itself out of existence, and after the smashed opera hats and ruined conventions had been cleared away, it was found that something new had come into being. It was becoming known as café society.

Like any other social manifestation, café society was

evolved over a considerable period of time and as the result of a number of otherwise unrelated forces, motives, and circumstances. It existed in its purest form in New York and New York's closest suburb, Hollywood.

It had its counterpart in what were known as the "bright young people" of London. Its first authentic flowering was in the speakeasy age of the twenties, but its full-blown maturity came with Repeal and mass entertainment in public resorts.

There had been signs and portents as far back as the nineties that the impeccable respectability, or at least the superficial conventionality, of the Edith Wharton era was in a decline. The most historic of these was an event ever since known as the "Awful Seeley Dinner," a masculine foregathering which to-day would scarcely cause comment among the participants, but which in the brownstone Gotham of 1896 assumed the proportions and awful glory of a Babylonish revel.

It was discovered that at the ushers' dinner of Clinton Seeley, grandson of P. T. Barnum, served in a suite of private rooms at Sherry's, a dancer named "Little Egypt" had appeared before the guests in what, for those times, passed as the nude.

The dinner was raided by the celebrated Captain "Whiskers" Chapman of the Tenderloin Squad, an officer whose beard and umbrella—the latter carried in lieu of a nightstick—won him a kind of local immortality, and the resulting scandal surpassed all bounds of probability. The public prints, hitherto unaccustomed to indulging in details of this sort, were given full license by the court proceedings which followed, and the town was fascinated with the first complete coverage of a notorious interlude in the life of the foie-gras faubourgs. Forward-looking city editors and society reporters, up to that time restricted to anonymous paragraphs where names were suggested by initials and asterisks, or to conventional flattering chronicles of balls and private routs, began to see a great light.

Coincidental with the rise of journalism based on gossip and scandal, almost universal later, there awakened among the more responsible members of society some appreciation of the uses of publicity. Newspaper reporters were even admitted to drawing-rooms, although at such times a close watch was kept on the overcoat rack in the hall, and notables who had hitherto scorned the public prints began actually to smile at the camera from the boxes of coaches-and-four or behind the wheels of Pope Hartfords set for hair-raising dashes to roadhouses in the wilds of Pelham. Old standards and reticences were crumbling, and the stage was being set for the dominance of the professional celebrity.

As an abrupt contrast to the days of cotillions and carriage calls, let us look at a gathering of the notables of café society as it exploded itself across New York some years later. It was Elsa Maxwell's Red and White Ball in honor of Mrs. Vincent Astor. The scene was the Starlight Roof of the Waldorf, and the participants were just about every one who amounted to anything in café society. The entire cast of *Jubilee* had just run through a scene from that revue, in which Miss Maxwell had played herself in a broad, even venomous vein of satire. Two of the most expensive orchestras were playing alternately, so that dancing was continuous. Supper was being served: a hot madrilène, broiled quail, a mousse of foie gras, and pails, double magnums, tanks, reservoirs of vintage champagne.

Not only had the five hundred guests come in red-and-white devisings of their own: they had been provided with two complete changes of costume one to be donned at two o'clock and the other at four, an arrangement which was enough, what with the refreshments, to make any one only vaguely certain of his own identity by five in the morning. Nor were the costumes simple masks and head-dresses: they were elaborate and complete changes—dragoons, monks, ladies of the Middle Ages, bishops, frontiersmen, knights in armor and ladies in Directoire attire. A corps of valets and ladies' maids were in the dressing-rooms to assist the guests and to see that the original costumes were returned next day to their owners.

Stand-up bars at each end of the town's handsomest ballrooms served stags, and waiters with trays of champagne circulated constantly among the tables. There was a vast deal of drinking, of amiable laughter and uproar, but nobody in the crowd was really tight. At seven-thirty, when the bands stopped playing, there would be a few men who might be characterized as stiff, but not falling-down stewed.

The personnel of one of Miss Maxwell's parties represented the ultimate tops in New York celebrities. At one table there were Cole Porter, Tallulah Bankhead, William Gaxton, Mrs. William Randolph Hearst, the Tommy Suffern Tailers, and Mrs. Seton Porter. On the dance floor Julien Chaqueneau had for partner Lady Peel (Beatrice Lillie), while Ethel Merman was on the arm of Prince Serge Obolensky. At another table Mrs.

T. Markoe Robertson and Miss Gladys Swarthout were vis-à-vis with Harold Ross, editor of the *New Yorker,* and Alfred de Liagre, handsome and dashing young producer. Scattered over the premises were Margaret Pemberton, the Grand Duchess Marie, Eve Symington, Maury Paul, Clara Bell Walsh, Jerome Zerbe, Clifton Webb, Dwight Fiske, the Allan Ryans, John Hay Whitney, Stanley Walker, Arthur Train, and the Winthrop Aldriches. Miss Maxwell herself, plump, stubby, and cheerful was all over the place and knew every guest by his or her first name.

Membership in café society as a rule presupposed sufficient personal means to support a presentable metropolitan scheme of living, although many familiar figures in its midst might come by their keep in oblique ways. The limousined mistress, the handsome gigolo, and the pensioner-friend had recently returned to the scene in increasing numbers. But the dominant requisite for membership in the loosely coördinated circle of café society was a name that was news, a warrant for existence.

Every one had to be able to point to some occupation, achievement, distinction, or even notorious frailty that made identification possible. The person might be a painter, a press-agent, a lover of uncommon appeal, a film actress, the president of an aviation company, the principal patron of a particular restaurant, a society photographer, a professional hostess, or a night-club promoter. The old generalities of "clubman," "millionaire," "society woman," and "internationally known figure in the world of art and politics," were no longer meaningful, valid, or acceptable.

The recruits of café society stemmed from a number of sources, but its principal luminaries were of the generation that achieved maturity in the era following World War I. Whether or not its members fitted into so nice a chronological category, a general definition of café society might have been: an unorganized but generally recognized group of persons whose names made news and who participated in the professional and social life of New York available to those possessed of a certain degree of affluence and manners.

Never before was it so true that names made news. Perhaps the most influential single factor in the creation and shaping of a new urban order was the appearance of what, for lack of a more precise phrase, came to be known as personal journalism: gossip writers, columnists, and Manhattan-color paragraphers. A generation before, society reporters had chronicled the more stately aspects of social functions with a solicitous regard for the sensibilities of all concerned, and nice folk had usually broken into type only on such recognizedly respectable occasions as birth, marriage, and death.

But in 1937 the possessors of names that were news woke up on Monday morning, or sat up till the first editions of the *Daily Mirror* appeared Sunday night, to discover their most intimate secrets and emotions a matter of public knowledge in the column of Walter Winchell, and were vastly flattered and gratified. "Ah, I see you made Winchell this morning!" was a Manhattan salutation usually conveyed with respectful admiration bordering on envy, no matter what the context or editorial implication of the mention itself.

"My dear, Mr. Winchell says that George was thrown

out of the Stork Club and that I'm going to have a
blessed event! Isn't it heavenly?" a young matron tele-
phoned a friend one exciting Monday.

The contrast in the attitude toward publicity of
horse-cab and side-whiskers society and café society was
not the least outstanding difference between the two
orders. Personal gossip was by no means the invention
of Walter Winchell, but he lent the retailing of spicy
news a bright new technic when he first started his column in the *Evening Graphic* in the early twenties, and
he was the first practitioner of a style later widely and
sometimes successfully imitated. Other New York columns specializing in Broadway and café paragraphs con-
cerning the private lives of the famous included those
of Leonard Lyons in the New York *Post*, Ed Sullivan
and John Chapman in the *Daily News*, Louis Sobol in
the *Journal*, Whitney Bolton and Dorothy Dey in the
Morning Telegraph, and George Ross in the *World-
Telegram*.

Their sources of information were usually jealously
guarded, and the most difficult of all the problems which
confronted the average columnist was the verification
of the more exciting items that came to his desk. This
had somehow to be encompassed without direct con-
sultation of the individuals concerned, for there was a
universal inclination to deny everything, even among
folks who later were vastly pleased to find themselves
in the public prints. Then, too, the paragrapher had to
weigh every motive of his informers, since spite, jeal-
ousy, financial and business implications, professional
promotion, and the publicizing of self and friends could
be detected in the reports of even the most trusted spies.

Sources of information were jealously guarded

Louis Sobol, recognized as the dean of afternoon-paper paragraphers, was the despair of rivals and the wonder and admiration of his colleagues, if only for the incredible territory he contrived to cover. A mousy little man with horn-rimmed glasses, a big nose, and a nice taste in Shetland and cheviot suits, he managed to fill five columns a week of two thousand words each with names, news, anecdotes, color, and comment that was invariably fresh and, in its field, important. Half a dozen cocktail parties, dinner at "21" or Jack Dempsey's or La Hiff's Tavern, a first night fairly awash with celebrities, glamour, and good copy, a visit to two different Forty-fifth Street bars at the intermissions, and finally a tour of the night clubs which would include Leon and Eddie's, El Morocco, the Stork, the Kit Kat, the Cotton Club, and the Onyx were his standardized nightly routine before he sought out his Greenwich Village apartment and sat down to his typewriter. Nobody knew how he did it.

Too, Sobol enjoyed a considerable popularity with his professional associates, as he consistently refused to run items of news, witticism, or correction at the expense of other newspapermen. He felt that airing the soiled linen of his own calling was not the proper function of the working press. Various other paragraphers had no such standard of integrity.

In the case of fashionable entertainment and the social activities of the café set, it might safely be asserted that the type of reporting of these aspects of the Manhattan scene which prevailed then was an obvious result, rather than a motivating cause. When entertaining was a private affair privately conducted for the pleasure of people one knew, it was possible for a hostess such as Mrs. Fish, Mrs. Astor, Mrs. Alexandre, or Mrs. Gould to give out only what details she considered suitable for publication. But in a generation whose dinner parties, after-theater suppers and dances were conducted in public restaurants, in night clubs, or in the ballroom suites of luxury hotels, the antics, manners, and departures from decorum of the guests were easily chronicled.

The focal point of New York's entertaining was no longer the noble Vanderbilt mansion on Fifth Avenue, nor was it the drawing-rooms of Mrs. Hamilton McK. Twombly and Mrs. Orme Wilson or the opera box of Miss Annie Burr Jennings. It was probably the front-second-floor restaurant of Jack and Charlie's in Fifty-second Street, or the intimate gold-and-blue bar of the Colony Restaurant, or the postage-stamp floor at El Morocco, that glittering synthesis of a Cecil B. De Mille opium dream and a paragrapher's heaven. Nor were the head-lined performers any longer Mrs. William Watts Sherman, Mrs. Robert Goelet, and Miss Louise Iselin, even though these amiable and distinguished ladies were still featured as opera-box holders and in the reports of the Society for Improving the Conditions of the Poor.

The names in neons outside the show were more apt to be those of Woolworth Donahue, Robert Benchley, Mrs. Brock Pemberton, Libby Holman Reynolds, Noel Coward, Tallulah Bankhead, or the Louis Bromfields, some of whom were associated with the theater and only a few of whom would have appeared on Ward McAllister's celebrated list for Mrs. Astor's ball.

The transition from private balls and dinner parties

of three hours' duration, from the Metropolitan Opera, cotillions, supper parties in private homes, and the various levees like the Charity Ball, to public appearances of the socially prominent at restaurant and night-club parties, to the cocktail routes of such wits as Dwight Fiske and Clifton Webb and their chronicling in the newspaper columns next day, really required only fifteen years. Dates became casual, to be kept or broken on the whim of the moment; dinner receded from a flood tide of Burgundy and innumerable game courses and entrées to a simple four courses and champagne in double magnums; formality became a thing of the past in almost every field save that of personal attire, where standards remained much the same as they had always been among people of breeding and circumstance.

It was this amiably demented whirl of scrammy entertainments, Elsa Maxwell levees, Fifty-second Street morris dancing, whoopsing, screaming, and clogging it to Eddie Duchin music at the Persian Room of the Plaza, making pretty faces for the cameramen at Gilbert Miller first nights, bicycling through Central Park to charity carnivals, keeping luncheon trysts at the Vendôme in Hollywood and being at the old desk next morning, gossiping by the hour on the London phone, and living in a white tie till six of a morning before brushing the teeth in a light Moselle and retiring to bed, which constituted the life of Manhattan's café society.

It was a strenuous business, and right thinkers and forward lookers said it would end in nothing good. Said New York: Live half as long; see twice as much!

9

THEIR NAMES MADE NEWS

THE glamour which surrounded New York's café society derived, more than anything else, from the willingness of its celebrities to be constantly on parade. The names that made news were those of individuals whose lives visibly typified all the romance of urban civilization. They lived in luxury hotels, dined in restaurants and night clubs whose opulence had become a legend, and made no pretense of hiding their million-candle-power light under any bushel whatsoever.

Never before, probably, had New York been snowed under by such a blizzard of money as was then drifting through its streets, piling up at its night clubs and in the ateliers of its court jewelers, furriers, couturiers, and luxury tradesmen. Mink coats at forty thousand dollars became a commonplace. There was a rare perfume on the market priced—and selling—at five hundred dollars for an ounce flask. There was a positive shortage of matched sables and chinchilla; diamond boutonnières for men were being passed over the counter at

ten thousand dollars a copy; waiter captains were playing the market once more, and it was possible for two
to dine at the Colony and have very little change out of
a half-century bank note.

Let us select at random from the ranks of the town's
café society a few individuals and institutions that were
a part of the glittering scene.

Because he was so cosmopolitan as to be as much a
New Yorker as a Londoner, we shall take Noel Coward,
actor, playwright, musician, accomplished and versatile
artist in half a score of mediums. Mr. Coward was the
ranking professional celebrity of the English-speaking
world. He spent about twelve weeks of every year in
New York, and the term of his stay might well have
been known as the Coward Season. The smart activities
of the town revolved around his presence, his newest
play, his latest witticism or cocktail party, almost to the
exclusion of all other manifestations of daily life.

Mr. Coward had not always been the richest man of
the Anglo-American theater. He once came very close
to starvation in a midtown garret, and he might well
never have been heard from except for the friendship
of Alfred Lunt and Lynn Fontanne, who weren't so
well off themselves at the time, but who still could have
an unknown but ambitious English boy in for dinner
two or three times a week and give him the key to their
apartment when they were on the road.

The success of Mr. Coward's plays, his own stage appearances, his songs, like "Mad Dogs and Englishmen"
and "Some Day I'll Find You," and his limitless personal charm and enthusiasm for going places, doing
things, and being fascinating to every one he met were

the component parts in a rags-to-riches romance which had no counterpart in the contemporary theater.

While he was no night-club rounder, there was seldom a private party of account which Mr. Coward missed during his annual New York interlude, and if he could be induced by his hostess to sit down at the piano and play a few of his long-familiar but ever-popular songs, the evening became a part of history.

The hold that Mr. Coward exerted on the imaginations and loyalties of a vast and sophisticated following was chiefly attributable to that elusive quality, "charm." To him the world was an immense gag, sometimes wistfully sentimental, sometimes pathetic, but never to be treated too seriously. Amazingly youthful of person (only in his middle thirties), he had been known to hold such a difficult audience as New York's Dutch Treat Club—a convocation of cynical, show-us advertising men and executives—spellbound by the adroitness of his patter. He made fun of everything, himself first of all, and was, at heart, the kindest person imaginable.

"Marie Grand Duchess, 30 Beekman Pl." was the way she was listed in the telephone directory, and if you had been of a mind to chat personally with the first cousin of the late Czar, daughter of the Grand Duke Paul, sister of the Grand Duke Dmitri, Marie Pavlovna, ranking Russian exile of the United States, there would have been nothing to prevent you from dialing her number. Or you might have visited her at her commercial photography studio, where she made camera studies of persons, flowers, jewels, perfume bottles, evening wraps, or fashionable hairdresses.

In the Grand Duchess Marie was most dramatically

visible the synthesis of economic necessity, professional competence, and social assurance that made for recognition in café society.

"My brains are of more use to me than my title," the Grand Duchess was fond of saying, "and conditions have changed so much in recent years that society has grown to respect personal effort more than any other qualification in the individual." And this adequately summed up the requirements of professional society.

In appearance, Marie lived up to the most exacting expectations of what a Grand Duchess should be. Tall, brown-haired, and with a gait and carriage slightly on the imperial side, she was no razzle-dazzle figure in the night clubs, no overexploited ringside spectator at the town's gilded and less inhibited carnivals. She was chary of her person, preferring to lunch at the Colony with intimates—Prince Serge Obolensky, perhaps, or Princess Ketto Mikeladze—and to dine at home in her Beekman Place apartment with its walls covered with autographed photographs of royal and otherwise notable or noble celebrities.

She was at her best on such evenings as the Russian Naval Ball, the celebration of the Russian New Year the second week in January, and the ball of the Corps des Pages, when, under the influence of gleaming candlelight, old Slavic tunes, and the flow of vodka and champagne, something of the atmosphere of other times was recreated in the ballroom of the Plaza, and the one-time officers of the Czar in their skirted coats, high Cossack boots, daggers, and ribboned orders, performed the Sword Dance.

For nearly a decade, Marie had been the town's rank-

ing member of Continental nobility and a personage
without whose name no list of charity patrons, art sponsors, or ball guests was complete. By refraining from
facile commercial exploitation of her title and person,
she maintained a degree of dignity in keeping with her
charm, integrity, and horse sense.

Another café celebrity of major importance was
Robert Benchley, who was half the year a writer and
actor for the overlords of Hollywood and the other half
the drama reviewer for the *New Yorker*. Mr. Benchley
was the archetypal Hollywood-New York commuter,
ferrying himself casually across the continent aboard the
Chief or one of the Union Pacific's new streamliners,
lunching with Edith Wilkerson or Jock Whitney at the
Vendôme in Hollywood one day and three evenings
later turning up for dinner at Jack and Charlie's with
the striking and beautifully gowned Louise Macy (after-
wards to become Mrs. Harry Hopkins of White House
fame), who was one of the smartest dress designers of the
time and a sister of Mrs. Nicholas S. Ludington of Ard-
more, Pennsylvania, and Santa Barbara.

Mr. Benchley was one of the foremost of Manhattan's
gourmets, a kitchen inventor in his own right. A fixture
at "21," he was usually installed between the tables of
Herbert Bayard Swope, horse-race enthusiast and one-
time managing editor of the old *World,* and the gilded
Mrs. Henry Field of Chicago, aviatrix, big-game hunter,
and trespasser in a dozen fields of adventure previously
regarded as masculine preserves. Actors feared no critical
wit more than that of Mr. Benchley, who inquired,
when Leslie Howard followed his highly successful appearance in *The Petrified Forest* with a dismally pedes-

trian *Hamlet:* "Did you see Mr. Howard in *The Petrified Hamlet?*"

For the better part of a decade the brownstone mansion with the floriated iron grille and gateway, sunken entrance, and seasonal window boxes, known as Jack and Charlie's, had been one of the four or five most distinguished restaurants in town. Its address was 21 West Fifty-second Street.

It was as a restaurant and bar that "21" had its primary reason for existence, but its fame derived from the fact that its modest façade concealed a celebrity hideaway which had only three rivals in the United States: the Colony Restaurant, El Morocco, and the Vendôme Restaurant on Sunset Boulevard, Hollywood.

There was nothing about the exterior of Jack and Charlie's to distinguish it from the other resorts which made West Fifty-second the Rue de la Fontaine of America. Nor was the interior particularly palatial. There was a lounge tastefully furnished in green and white, with an open fire, a divan or two, and a rack of English sporting periodicals and daily papers. Beyond that was an oak-timbered taproom with a semicircular bar, and above this were two restaurants, at the front and back of the house. A white wooden-railed stairway lined with green carpet led upstairs, and there were a barbershop, a gymnasium, and the usual retiring and powdering rooms. Nothing else. Nothing, that is, but the clientele.

If you were a recognized and approved patron of the house, as soon as you stepped in the door, Jimmy, the concierge, said, "Good morning, sir" or "Good evening" as the case might be, and half a dozen sleek youths bustled forward to take your hat and coat. If Jimmy didn't look up from his desk nobody made any move in your direction, and if you persisted further in trying to be recognized and attended, Jimmy remarked with an infinity of sorrow in his voice that the house was filled to capacity and that there were no reservations to be made.

Now and then, of course, folk did get into "21" who weren't particularly wanted. For them there was a back room known as the "doghouse" and a special menu on which all the items were just double the prices on the regular card. The management comprised Jack and Mac Kriendler and Charlie Berns. Of this triumvirate, more later.

If you stepped into the bar to see who was on the premises one noon in the thirties, one, or rather, two of the first things you would see would be the twin beards, red and gray respectively, of Ernest Boyd, litterateur and boulevardier extraordinary, and Edgar Montillion Woolley, director of the production of *Fifty Million Frenchmen* and theater celebrity of the first order. If he was in town, Cole Porter, composer of innumerable hit songs, would be with Mr. Woolley. Ranged farther along the bar were Alfred G. Vanderbilt, invariably talking horse; Jefferson Machamer, the illustrator; Hal Phyfe, foremost of the town's professional photographers; Prince George Shebatoff; Steve Hannagan, ace press-agent; Morton Downey; Ernest Hemingway; John McClain, top-notch ship-news reporter for the New York *American* and friend of more international celebrities than you could shake a gold-headed stick at; Dudley Field Malone, noted divorce lawyer and one-time Collector of the Port of New York; Keats Speed, managing editor of the *Sun;* Damon Runyon, and Arthur Cooley, champagne salesman and husband of Marion Cooley, the professional night-club hostess.

Nowhere was there any suggestion of ostentatious luxury, but there was that intangible thing called "atmosphere" about the front restaurant upstairs. It was visible in the dexterity of the waiters; in the silver mesh of wine baskets and the sheen of champagne coolers at every table; in the masterful eye of Philip, the maître d'hôtel, and in the accomplished gestures of his captains, whether they were spreading Parmesan on your marmite Henri IV or achieving a Pain's fireworks effect with oranges and cognac over a flaming platter of crêpes Suzette. Wine corks were never permitted to pop too loudly; dessert appeared at just the proper interval after the salad and mousse of foie gras; the Armagnac was served in sniffing glasses big enough for the unwary to fall into.

This was luncheon hour of a no-matinée day, and there was a good representation of theater folk visible. At the center table just inside the door were Noel Coward and Gertrude Lawrence, sharing pompano and fresh asparagus with Jack Wilson, Mr. Coward's producer and business manager, and the amazing Princess Paley, to whom Mr. Wilson had been paying chivalrous attentions for several seasons. At the next table were Mrs. Brock Pemberton, wife of the producer and hostess at the town's most representative cocktail levees, with Dick Aldrich, lanky Harvard graduate and producer in his own right, and round-faced Donald Oenslager, whose stage sets were visible in no fewer than six Broadway hits during one season.

Elsewhere, busy with alligator pears, crabmeat au gratin, and slim bottles of Steinberger-Auslese '21, were Lois Long, former wife of Peter Arno and "Lipstick" on the staff of the *New Yorker;* Alice Leone Moats, the writer, with Burford Lorimer, son of the former editor of the *Saturday Evening Post;* Ted Husing, ace radio announcer; James Montgomery Flagg, the illustrator; Nancy Randolph of the *Daily News,* with Joseph John O'Donohue IV, gilded Park Avenue youth; and Frank Sullivan and Corey Ford, humorists, magazine writers, and the closest of professional associates.

To trace the emergence of a group of tavern proprietors who became such important factors in the café society scene that their influence could not be ignored by any amateur of social evolution, it is necessary to go back to the dark days of the early twenties, the Ordovician Age of speakeasy geology.

Café society came into being in the form in which it was finally recognized, through the agency of the speakeasies, and a small handful of their more far-sighted, ambitious, and urbane proprietors were, in a way, the arbiters of its earlier destinies.

The first of the speakeasies to command a national reputation and a clientele of reputable patrons was Dan Moriarty's famous men's bar at 216 East Fifty-eighth Street. Dan and his two brothers, Mort and Jim, were the salt of the earth. They were influential citizens on the upper East Side, where they owned large real estate holdings.

Their unostentatious bar, located in the basement of

a brownstone house, became known as a safe and respectable resort of masculine fashion. The liquor was the best obtainable in a dangerous time; the premises were free from police molestation and all but the most infrequent Federal raids; and no shady characters, toughs, or ugly drunks were allowed inside the door. Dan was banker, confidant, bail bondsman, and friend to half the distinguished blades of the town.

Of an evening youths were accustomed to run over to Dan's from the balls and debutante parties at the luxury resorts along Park Avenue. The bar was populated with snowy shirt-fronts and gleaming top hats set at the rakish angle. The place became a sort of outpost of the Racquet and Tennis Club, the Union League, the Yale Club, and Harvard's aristocratic Porcellian all rolled into one.

Every one who was any one was there of an evening: it was the regular resort of Paul Palmer, then editor of the *American Mercury;* of Sherman Hoyt, most famous of all American yachtsmen, who was accustomed to wear oilskins and a sou'wester over his tails on stormy nights; of Jim Williamson, who drew the Kelly-Springfield advertisements; of Peter Arno, then a Yale undergraduate, and of his classmates, John Hay Whitney, Avery Rockefeller, Count Henri de Sibour, and Rudy Vallee. To be a member of the regulars at Dan's was the equivalent of being a recognized fixture at White's or one of the dandy coffee houses of eighteenth-century London.

Dan's youngest brother, Jim, a tall, handsome, redheaded Irishman, was a great favorite with the younger men across the bar. He used to spar with some of them in his nicely appointed flat down the street and, after

hours, went on parties with them to the Jungle or the
Dizzy Club or the other favorite night clubs of the
moment. One always sent Jim greetings at Christmas
and New Year's, and post-cards from abroad.

One day, either as a good-natured gesture or with
serious intent—it was never known which—a Yale youth
persuaded his sister to send Jim an invitation to her
coming-out party at Sherry's. It was a salient moment
in the history of New York society when the majordomo at Sherry's announced, "Mr. James Moriarty,"
and Jim, attired in what was then known as a "Tux"
and smiling a handsome Irish smile, passed down a receiving line of opera-length gloves, lorgnettes, and blazing necklaces.

To say that he achieved a success would be understatement. He was a born dancer, pleased with himself
as a puppy with a bone, and the personal friend of every
man on the floor. The times took no account of the
circumstance that he was a barkeep: it was the jazz
age, and all that people demanded of him was that he
be a good one.

From that time on, Jim was a figure in the night
clubs, a sort of social character, and eventually, feeling
the urge for higher things, he shook the sawdust of his
brother's speakeasy from his feet and started a restaurant in Sixty-first Street right across from the marquee
of the ultra-swank Pierre's.

It was the age that saw the rise of East Side Tony, of
West Side Tony, of Steve and Ed Bozzonetti and of innumerable Albertos, Umbertinos, and Boscaglios, and
in the midst of a spring tide of the most dreadful liquor
ever destined for human consumption, a few forward-

looking individuals began to see possibilities which were to bring them affluence and recognition.

Among them were an Italian named John Perona, who was running a speakeasy in West Forty-ninth Street just a block off Fifth Avenue; Jack Kriendler and Charlie Berns, who had set up a rival hideaway called the Puncheon Grotto directly across the street from Perona, and Sherman Billingsley, an engaging young man whose celebrated Stork Club of to-day had numerous predecessors by the same name in various parts of town during the Great Foolishness.

These admirably forethoughtful restaurateurs probably had no prevision of Repeal. It is doubtful if any one had at that time, but the service of liquor in New York had become an established and permanent industry, and these particular individuals, having an eye to the carriage trade and a pride in their calling, found themselves, toward the latter half of the twenties, serving nothing but uncut, imported, and veritable liquors, the finest vintage wines, and food of a comparable quality.

There began to be a certain prestige in lunching and dining at these smart resorts. Already the Messrs. Kriendler, Berns, Perona, and Billingsley were building up a clientele whose snob appeal and names were to be an inestimable asset with Repeal. All they had to do was to get a license and throw away the bolt on the front door.

The last three or four years of the thirties saw a great revival of the luxury hotel and restaurant trade in premises once permeated by legality and gloom, and a number of smaller but infinitely smart restaurants such as the Colony, Jean's French delicatessen in Sixtieth Street, the Aperitif, run by Leon and Gregory, and Theodore Titze's Theodore's, came into a renewed prosperity.

Most exacting in the selection of its patrons, most breath-takingly costly in its tariff, and far and away the smartest restaurant between the East and North rivers, the Colony was a screen director's dream of fashionable celebrities on dress parade. From the intimate premises of its ivory-and-blue brocade bar and from the knowing and grave courtesy of its wine steward in his gold chain of office, there distilled a flattering atmosphere of exclusiveness and well-being which attracted gourmets, grand duchesses, and stage stars as a saucer of extra Grade A cream does kittens.

George Jean Nathan dined there almost nightly with Miss Mai-Mai Sze, orchidaceous daughter of the Chinese Ambassador. Whitney Bourne, stunning society girl of the stage, was frequently visible there with her tail-coated and opera-cloaked cavalier of the moment. Cecil Beaton, favored photographer of celebrities, lunched almost daily with Elsa Maxwell, whiplash-witted arbiter of social revels.

The Grand Duchess Marie and the monocled Prince George of Russia bowed across to a table where Vinton Freedley, most soigné and urbane of theatrical producers, was busy with breast of guinea hen Eugénie, a magnum of Bollinger '26, British market, and the anecdotes of Clara Bell Walsh, who possessed and, what's more, wore the most eye-popping rubies in town.

The seating of patrons at the Colony, under the infinitely wise direction of Gene, the proprietor, was the most arbitrary this side of the pew list of St. Thomas'

Church on Fifth Avenue. The right-hand corner table nearest the door was for years the special location of William K. Vanderbilt. Other reservations were those of Beth Leary, a veteran first nighter and hostess of the town, William Rhinelander Stewart, and Ellin Mackay Berlin, daughter of the satrap of Postal Telegraph and wife of the foremost of popular songwriters.

In general, the more revered patrons were seated nearer the door, and the portion of the restaurant behind the half-partition hung with heavy crimson damask was known as the "monkey house." A table to the left of the entry and quite in the middle of the restaurant floor—often occupied by Marlene Dietrich—was as much of a greeters' rendezvous as a location for dining. So necessary was it for its gentlemen occupants to stand while their companions chatted with passing acquaintances that eating was relegated to the background.

Emphasis at the Colony was more upon food and wine than at either Jack and Charlie's or El Morocco and, generally speaking, within its portals business was strictly in abeyance. Film moguls just off the Century, British novelists still dazed from an early docking of the *Queen Mary,* and other topnotchers in New York on matters of professional urgency were rushed by their agents to lunch at "21," where, in an atmosphere of highly geared enterprise and with table telephones ready to be plugged in on Hollywood or London, business could be transacted with a minimum of friction.

But the Colony was a temple of gastronomy alone. Its *raison d'être* was found primarily in its roast grouse, fresh from Scotch moors, its rare Burgundies, and its

rolling bar stocked with most of the liqueurs known
to man.

The real estate trend which transformed all but the
very richest Manhattanites into apartment- or hotel-
dwellers ended the long tradition of home entertainments on a magnificent scale. Cocktail parties and small

Fame came in tabloid form

dinners were the only generally observed types of private parties to survive.

New York, of course, had always lunched in public,
and great debutante parties had for years been held by
tradition at the Ritz, Sherry's, Pierre's, or the Colony
Club. Now New York society was getting accustomed
to doing everything of an entertaining nature in public.

Publicity, too, was becoming a valuable commodity,
and editors preferred pictures and names of actresses,
screen stars, and radio celebrities, who knew from their
professional experience how to make news and how to

pose, to the blank expressions and maladroit utterances of the average debutante. Dwight Fiske, Eve Symington, Cobina Wright, and other professional entertainers and entrepreneurs with plush overtones suddenly discovered that the social activities of New York were revolving about them and their friends and acquaintances, and that the actual individuals of the Social Register, unless they were amusing, successful in their own right, and amenable to changing times and institutions, were headed for oblivion.

Close upon the heels of society's emergence from the mists of privacy and exclusiveness came the reporters, paragraphers, and columnists, and behind them came the photographers. No longer was it even plausible for folk of fashion to shield themselves from the flash-lights as they scurried across the sidewalk. A few old-fashioned irreconcilables still affected the gesture, and often as not actually didn't get snapped for their pains, a contingency which never failed to make them furious.

The first "candid" cameraman to get exclusive shots of notables in Manhattan's café society was Jerome Zerbe, who was retained by Editor Harry Bull of *Town and Country* to procure photographs of celebrities in moments of unconventional intimacy. So great was Mr. Zerbe's success that within two years half a score of imitators had sprung up. The only one to parallel his success was Marty Black of the New York *American,* but close behind them were Tony Sarno of International News, Gloria Braggiotti, fashion expert of the New York *Post* and photographic free lance, and a youth named Dan McNutt. In Hollywood Hyman Fink was an established social fixture among the stars.

The lensman became a not inconsiderable figure in
the social midst. Tail-coated and top-hatted of an evening, his presence was solicited at the best tables at any
party, and the cocktail shebang or dinner dance at
which no press photographer was present was considered an unequivocal failure by host and guests alike.

The ultimate hallmark of social success in the Manhattan of 1937 was a four-column cut of one's self in the
American, posed against the distinguishing zebra stripes
of the Morocco décor, with a cooler of wine on one's
table and an eligible companion. The credit line would
read, "Photo by Black," and the implications of achievement in the New York parade were precisely those
which, a generation before, reposed in the chaste script
lettering of a card reading, "Mrs. Vanderbilt re-
quests...."

Take a gander at one of the more sensational barn
raisings of the era.

Unlimited quantities of champagne were poured
freely at the bar. Ray Bolger, star revue dancer, whisked
around the ballroom floor with Edith Gray, sister of
the Dowager Duchess of Marlborough, who was dressed
in a milkmaid's costume and wearing more than $100,-
000 worth of diamond and emerald bracelets.

Mrs. "Mudge" Howard, who was in trade and knew
everybody in Manhattan by his or her first name, was
in a vague parody of rustic clothes and wearing the
Howard pearls, which were by way of being something.
There was a papier-mâché cow bedded down on real
straw in a stall in the corner opposite the most expensive orchestra available.

"What," you gasped, seizing the arm of a passing

wine steward, "what in the name of holy hoopskirts is it all about?"

It was Elsa Maxwell's "Barnyard Frolic" on the Starlight Roof of the Waldorf-Astoria, Park Avenue, New York—that's what it was. And it was attended by every café society celebrity who could possibly beg, wrangle, or borrow an invitation to the season's most dazzling costume ball.

Lady Iya Abdy, spectacular Russo-British beauty, had on red tights and a headdress made of a very dead stuffed crow. Prince Serge Obolensky, in peasant garb, led a fat, squealing pig on an expensive dog leash. Mrs. James A. Corrigan, who had outgrown Cleveland society and who had preferred that of King Edward VIII until he became overnight the Duke of Windsor, was dressed as a Russian moujik, but with an enormous emerald set in twenty-carat diamonds on one arm and three ropes of Oriental pearls around her neck. Mrs. Ogden L. Mills wore a blinding diamond tiara above blue-denim overalls.

Leonard Hanna, Cleveland multimillionaire, had imported a genuine Ohio hog caller, who was making his strange native cries heard above Fairchild's new swing band, and Mr. and Mrs. Douglas Fairbanks, Constance Bennett, and Gilbert Roland were in identical farmer suits, looking for all the world like a group of synthetic rustic quadruplets.

It would take two full columns of news space to list all the people who attended one of Miss Maxwell's more pretentious parties, but a few more of those participating in this parody barn dance were the Fredric Marches of Hollywood; Lauritz Melchior of the Metropolitan

Opera; Princess Natalie Paley; Oliver Messel, English
theatrical scene designer; Mario Braggiotti, the band
leader; Harry Payne Bingham; George Jean Nathan,
the drama critic; Mrs. Vincent Astor; Charlie MacArthur, of the famed Hollywood team of Hecht and Mac-
Arthur; Beatrice Lillie, fresh from her performance in
The Show Is On; Winthrop Aldrich; Averell Harriman
of the Union Pacific, and Cornelius Vanderbilt Whitney, cousin of the famous Jock Whitney.

For Elsa Maxwell, short, snub-nosed, and almost as
frumpy in her attire as the late Hetty Green, was the
ranking hostess of two continents and sponsored the
New York parties which were the 1937 equivalents of
the balls and cotillions of Mrs. Astor in the mustache-
cup era.

Her parties were vast and inclusive and were tre-
mendously publicized. About the only similarity between Miss Maxwell's routs and the stately parties of
a generation before was their hold on the public imagination, but there is no denying that they were the
parties of that moment, and very magnificent parties
they were, too.

A plain girl, stemming from California, with little to
recommend her but a talent for playing the piano, Miss
Maxwell blossomed, in the years after the war, into an
entrepreneur of festivities whose ambitions carried her
into the charmed circle of European royalty and later
to fame as the arbiter of New York's top-drawer revelry.
Getting a start among the bored and wealthy sophisti-
cates who lounged in the corridors and cafés of the
Paris Ritz and were too lazy and unimaginative to ar-

range their own entertainments, she soon succeeded, through her wit, creative sense, authoritative mannerisms, and sheer brass in securing the patronage of world notables, in elevating herself to a social eminence nobody could afford to ignore.

During the days of suffrage crusading, Miss Maxwell had been a protégée of the imposing Mrs. O. H. P. Belmont. The real Maxwell saga, however, begins after the war and at the Lido, where she contrived to be the first to introduce Noel Coward and Queen Marie of Romania to the beach-pavilion and swimming-shorts set. She inaugurated a night club that made night hideous aboard a barge which floated around Venice.

A chronicler of the Maxwell legend asserts that though the then Prince of Wales came to her parties, he never had a really good time because no Englishman likes to be told how to manage his own fun, and the management of her guests was Miss Maxwell's most dominant qualification as a hostess. At Biarritz she gave the first of the internationally celebrated "treasure hunts," which ended in the swimming pool of a famous couturière, where every one plunged in fully dressed to get the treasure.

She was retained by the management at Monte Carlo to draw the American trade during the opulent twenties and told the director the first thing he'd have to install was a rubber bathing beach, because the crazy Americans were used to the best of everything. Her most magnificent essay in the realm of spacious gestures was at a party given for her at the Paris Ritz. Her host gallantly offered her a five-thousand-dollar gem as a place card, but she refused it in favor of having Kreisler play for her guests after the cognac.

Her all-time high in the field of al fresco entertaining was a party at Luxor, Egypt, where the guests were transported to dinner in the desert aboard camels which jounced them so that, as one celebrity remarked, all they had to do was swallow straight gin and both kinds of vermouth, which instantly became shaken into a perfect Martini.

Then there were professional hostesses who were part of the Manhattan scene. There was, for instance, Mrs. Cobina Wright, herself a singer of consequence, who undertook to procure the services of celebrities for radio hours and musical affairs. There was Marion Cooley, an adept at reviving night clubs and hotel cabarets whose patronage wasn't all it should have been. There was Katrinka Suydam Roelker, an expert in inaugurating cocktail lounges and intimate restaurants, and there was Mrs. Caresse Crosby, who thought up some of the most bafflingly madhouse shindigs New York has ever seen.

Perhaps the cream of lunatic parquet pounding and glass tossing was the party promoted a decade ago by Mrs. Crosby at the smart Coq Rouge Restaurant in honor of Salvador Dali, whom certain limited circles of hyper-esthetes believed to be a surrealist painter. Surrealism was to ordinary art what Latvian vodka was to dandelion wine and was calculated to affect the average person in much the same way.

Every one was to come to Mrs. Crosby's rout dressed as a dream. Mrs. James Roosevelt, appeared in a cellophane skirt, with a large bunch of carrots tied in her hair. Miss Louise Crane also affected a carrot motif, but went Mrs. Roosevelt one better by wearing a girdle, a necklace, and bracelets designed with this form of garden truck. They were considered very Dali indeed.

Madame Dali came as the Spirit of Necrophilia in a transparent red-paper skirt and with a headdress of papier-mâché, representing a child's head and torso, and a boiled lobster. Kirk Askew, a confirmed surrealist, appeared with his face covered with a mat of hairpins. Mrs. Harold Sterner represented "Falling Downstairs," her most persistent dream, by twining half a dozen snakes (stuffed) about her person.

A good deal of attention, not all of it favorable, was attracted by a typical Dali decorative note. On a table in the diametrical center of the dance floor reposed the large, raw carcass of a cow, with a phonograph where its internal economy had originally been, grinding out music of patently Negroid origin. It symbolized the falling-from-a-great-height dream, explained Monsieur Dali, who was neatly turned out with a glass case on his chest, in which was arranged a woman's brassiere.

Bronson Williams, the very social tailor, was immaculate in starched evening linen and broadcloth from the waist up, but from the waist down wore little more than a pair of women's black stockings supported by women's garters. Kermit Roosevelt just let it go with a two-faced mask, and William H. Labrot came in a large bath towel, explaining that his suppressed desire was to be Nero.

Another not-too-rational form of entertainment was arranged a short time later by Joe Ryle and Maida Cain, young promotion experts. This pair introduced the rotating or guzzle-and-gallop dinner. A large bus was cleared of seats, a dance floor laid down, and a band installed at one end and a bar at the other. In this rolling rendezvous the guests danced and drank cocktails en route to the first port of call, the smart Madison Restaurant.

Here they disembarked and sat down in the restaurant to the opening course of dinner, clear turtle soup with sherry. The fish course was served at Armando's, the entrée in the bar of the Lombardy, and so on, far, far into the night.

Marion Cooley, round, jolly, and apparently carefree, perfected a technic quite her own for establishing the reputations of cafés and night clubs. Mrs. Cooley had a phenomenally wide acquaintance among socially inclined New Yorkers and specialized in the staging of Sunday-night suppers of an informal and often hilarious nature. Her routs resembled amateur nights in the theater, and there was apt to be impromptu entertainment by the patrons themselves.

A typical turnout at one of Mrs. Cobina Wright's foregatherings included such names as those of the Grand Duchess Marie of Russia; Quentin Reynolds, the fiction and sports writer; Valentina Schlee, one of the town's most picturesque couturières; Myra Kingsley, dean of New York astrologers; Frank Chapman and his song-bird wife, Gladys Swarthout; Clifton Webb, of stage fame; Hal Phyfe and Horst, the photographers; Clara Bell Walsh, first nighter and art patron; Gene Tunney, the Connecticut squire; Gilbert and Alice Seldes; and Marion Tiffany Saportas, flaming-haired beauty and a distinguished hostess in her own right. Present, too, were Peggy Fears, wife of A. C. Blumenthal; Dwight Fiske, jongleur of fashionable salons; Edmund and Toni Anderson, perhaps the most frequently photographed of all night-club patrons; Paul Draper, youthful tap dancer, and his friend Mario Braggiotti; Moss Hart; Lois Long; Tallulah Bankhead; Freddy Beckman, playboy and husband of Jules Bache's daughter; Mrs. Brock Pemberton; Libby Holman Reynolds, and Alfred de Liagre, youthful producer of the hit, *Yes, My Darling Daughter.*

Others on the leash of the elite usually available for such occasions were Donald Ogden Stewart, the humorist; Beatrice Lillie, Morton Downey, Clare Boothe Brokaw Luce, Victor Moore, the comedian; Richard Knight, a noted divorce lawyer, and his wife; Nicolas de Molas and Cecil Beaton, fashionable foreign artists; Paul Flato, then a leading private jeweler; Sheila Barrett, society chanteuse, and Ben Hecht. Also Eddie Duchin, the handsome and fashionable orchestra leader; Johnny Weissmuller and Lupe Velez; Mr. and Mrs. Phil Ammidown; Randy Burke, café wit and familiar figure of the boulevards; Paul Gallico, sports writer; Shipwreck Kelly, baseball entrepreneur; Charles Hanson Towne, Ilka Chase, and Margalo Gilmore; Jo Mielziner, the stage designer; Howard Hughes; Rosamond Pinchot, and John O'Hara, author of *Butterfield 8.*

Of the town's three or four ranking resorts of professional society, Sherman Billingsley's Stork Club was most celebrated as a rendezvous of newspapermen, sports writers, and columnists. At its square bar were to be seen such Manhattanites as the omnipresent Walter Winchell; Damon Runyon, ace sports writer of the generation; Steve Hannagan, publicity exploiter, and

Louis Sobol. Richards Vidmer, sports columnist; Stanley Walker, legendary newspaperman, and, on occasion, Katharine Brush, most beautiful and soignée of writers of romances, might have been found in the back room with its diminutive dance floor.

Mr. Billingsley was distinguished as a night-club entrepreneur on a number of counts. He took the pains to maintain a cuisine whose Florida specialties, such as pompano and fresh stone crabs, were flown to his chefs by a daily airplane service. He was noted as the most generous host in town with newspapermen.

So far as the reporters of café-society folk were concerned, the conception of a newspaperman as an unshaven, shabby youth was as obsolete as hand-set type.

Maury Paul, known to the world as Cholly Knickerbocker and ranking white-tie reporter of the country, was a plump, laughing, and omnipresent pressman with a nice taste in diamond studs, a leaning toward sloe-gin rickeys, and a famous custom-body imported car. Mr. Paul could no more have attended all the functions to which he was asked than could President Roosevelt, and to have him actually present at dinner was a triumph for a hostess ranking with the entertainment of royalty.

And visible in this entertaining admixture of talents and personalities were representatives of a type which seldom before penetrated New York's glitter scene and never in such substantial numbers: the social adventurer. To be sure, Manhattan society of the era of gas lamps and villas at Newport was familiar with the titled foreigner in search of susceptible heiresses, and society of every age has been conscious of new-comers within its sphere. But café society was the first urban milieu into which complete strangers were welcomed if they had qualities to recommend them.

Every season the photographers' flashes revealed the emergence of numbers of youths whose primary and too often sole warrant for attention was good looks, a reasonable range of topical conversation, and a sufficiency of clean linen to don a white tie and waistcoat every evening. Their sole objective was entertainment, dinner at the Colony, and a bowing acquaintance with Tallulah Bankhead, and most of them achieved this reasonable end.

Is there, readers may ask, any conclusion to be drawn from the café scene of New York as it represented the dominance of a new social order?

This much at least is apparent: the café society of New York was infinitely more democratic, more open to achievement, than the older social order. The requirements for membership in it were primarily those of professional success, personal distinction, and willingness to subscribe to only the vaguest of formal codes. Almost anybody with something to offer stood an excellent chance of becoming somebody in café society.

Admission to the now obsolete and almost forgotten mysteries of formal society demanded neither character, charm, nor achievement, but presupposed, in most cases, substantial wealth and often required a period of probation extending over generations.

New York in 1937 was a city of luxurious resources never before so attainable by ambitious youth with something to give. Its motto might very well have been: "Here it is; come and get it."

10

BILTMORE BATHS

MORE obnoxious, perhaps, than any other subject which by continued repetition distressed us during a juvenile career in a number of the better preparatory schools was that phase of history which was devoted to a discussion of the debts of modernity to the ancients. And of all the ancients the Romans were incalculably the most offensive, by reason of the extent of their gifts to subsequent generations and the necessity of memorizing this catalogue of boons and usufructs derived from their distressing competence in any number of fields of endeavor.

It was usually enough to know that medicine and mathematics were "developed" by the Mahometans, and that the Code of Hammurabi and a pretty obvious type of temple architecture was the contribution to civilization of the Assyrians. But the Romans were just a superlative headache. They did so much. There were governmental institutions, systems of architecture, the Latin language, all sorts of legal devices (most of which the world has not yet recovered from), philosophies, democratic principles, and even a system for licensing the lupinaria. Our attitude, however, is changing. We no longer resent the Code of Justinian. The members of the younger torts and misdemeanors set can have it and welcome, and now that we actually own a Pine's Horace our rage against the Latin language is more or less abated.

But what really, more than any other single factor, has accomplished our reconciliation with Rome is that most magnificent of institutions for which the Romans were actually responsible: the Turkish bath.

Just why the Turkish bath should have been so neglected by the historians of antiquity and palmed off as a Turkish invention along with Turkish paste, Turkish carpets, and Turkish coffee, not to mention an improbable kind of pipe which involves the use of rose water, we have never been able to understand. Certainly the hot baths were in common use among the best citizens of the Roman Mayfair long before the first bey ever languished in a steam room. But among historians a sort of prejudice against the institutions seems to have arisen. It can frequently be found listed among the causes of the downfall of the empire, along with the decline of the latafundia and the unfortunate practice of lionizing the Christians.

To be sure, then as now, the baths were undoubtedly frequented to a certain extent by rowdy people with tastes for oblique and exotic divertissement, and a perusal of Petronius in any of the franker translations will convince anybody that all the fun that was had was not of the good, clean variety. Whence, otherwise, the name bagnio? But by and large, the hot baths seem to have been, so far as most people are concerned, God's gift to a world quite fed up with such unimaginative devices as tubs and showers.

Next to godliness

Nor has the Turkish bath as an institution been accorded its proper place in literature. All historical novelists treating of classic times, such as Bulwer-Lytton and Sienkiewicz, to be sure have devoted an interlude or so to the tepidarium, and in our own time Mr. Arlen and Evelyn Waugh have not been impervious to the charm of steam room and frigidaria at the Jermyn Street Hammam, but in general the subject has never received adequate treatment from men of letters of the first rank.

To the Turkish bath addict it would be impossible to imagine any one to whom this most luxurious and casual of pastimes would not seem delightful, either as an alternative for exercise or as a sheer, gratuitous, and unprovoked indulgence of sybaritic tastes. Long ago we were ourself inaugurated into the mysteries of the steam room and the ineffable delight of reclining on spotless linen in the tepidarium, where the mercury hovers at 150, in the realm of Bob Kiphuth at Yale gymnasium, and to our untutored eye the crude fittings of the college thermae appeared the ultimate achievement in mechanical artistry. In those days, known as the Good Old Times (circa 1924), the steam room of the gym was of an afternoon a gathering place for academic wits and undergraduate intelligentsia rivaling the Elizabethan Club in College Street.

Later, when the bright young men of Yale discovered Paris, they simultaneously discovered the hammam at the Claridge in the Champs-Élysées, and for a time each July and August the New Haven symposium was continued here, materially assisted by the immediate proximity of the bar across the corridor. The amiable Bob Kiphuth gave daily gym classes for those who were able to stand and swing their arms with any reasonable degree of precision. By that time the spell was on us, and to-day the sign "Turkish bath" has the same effect on us that swinging doors are said to have had for an earlier generation, or a judas hole in a door had upon any normal person of a later rebellious era.

Nor are the charms of the hammam limited to mere

gratification of the senses alone. For the student of the human comedy there is opportunity for speculation on many aspects of mundane existence in the sight of the great and near great, devoid of the trappings of circumstance, gasping and puffing beneath the emphatic attentions of some hairy baboon of a rubber. For the moment he is master of judge, bishop, or merchant prince within the narrow confines of his stone-walled rubbing cubicle. The parade of pretentious humanity becomes for the interim but an allegory of flesh and futility, played in fantastic posturings to an accompaniment of hosings and slappings and the bellowings of outraged dignity.

Nor at any time do we experience such a sense of utter cleanliness and virtue as upon emerging, scoured, scalded, and rejuvenated, from the catharsis of salt and steam, a soul cleansed in a purgatory of needle sprays and electric cabinets more fearful of aspect than any contrivance of Dante's most robust imaginings. There is nothing in hell so satisfying as the sight of the pinguid features of one you know as an after-dinner speaker of note projecting from the flaming depths of an electric cabinet.

Probably the most notable of Manhattan's hammams is located deep in the innards of the Biltmore Hotel, where the mighty and the witty foregather, particularly of a Saturday afternoon, to purge themselves of Wilkens Family and the alcoholic oddments of nocturnal life. Former Governor Al Smith is sage and dean of the Biltmore; Jim Farley, the eminent politico, is prone to catch up on his week's reading of papers and periodicals at a favored spot in the remote corner of the tepidarium; Steve Hannagan, the publicist, makes a practice of recovering from wakes by alternate immersion in its steam room and in its ice showers; Gene Tunney can be discovered there on occasion, supplementing his rules of health with a brisk workout; Allan Jones, the boy thrush, is an aficionado, and Al Jolson plays the horses from its slightly claustrophobic phone booth. There are occasional alarms, as when bemused patrons sink to the bottom of the pool and fail to come to the surface of their own volition, but by and large life at the Biltmore is possessed of a gentling quality suited to the frayed nerves of its regulars.

Such is the sense of piety welling within the emergent patron of the steam rooms that it seems impossible that he should ever again fall into the ways of error. Crude fellows, far gone in wanton endeavor, cry out for Belindas and strong waters while dressing, but it is usually an hour or so before the sinner refreshed and redeemed can view a swinging door with anything save loathing.

11

SOUVENIRS OF THESPIS

A THEATER reporter mutters in his beard: The first play I ever saw was *Under Cover* at the Plymouth Theater in Boston—God knows how long ago—but I can recall the gunfire noises of the crook melodrama to this very red-hot minute. *Under Fire,* the war play, and *The Roundup* also loom large in retrospect, probably because they, too, were largely performed under a pall of black powder smoke which blew into the audience and smelled deliciously of slaughter. It's a silly New York fire regulation that restricts stage firearms to .22 caliber, although the machine-gun built by a stage carpenter for Humphrey Bogart in *The Petrified Forest* was pretty effective.

Seeing a nonesuch entitled *The Grand Duke,* in which an elegant pre-Monty Woolley actor with a fine beard sat before herring frozen into a cake of ice with just their tails protruding for his ducal breakfast, prompted me and my roommate at Yale to command a similar arrangement for breakfast on my twenty-first birthday. The result was less elegant but more exciting, since the New Haven Ice Company, more or less understandably, mistook the order and froze the herring solid in a mass in the middle of the cake of ice, and it had to be attacked and demolished with a fire ax before they were available for consumption along with a case of champagne wine secured from Andy Dunbrowsky, the campus bootlegger. The wine was strictly Hackensack Meadows, Private Cuvée, 1921.

I wonder how Keith Prowse, the London theater ticket brokers, are getting along. The name is so distinguished, like banking with Coutts' or having boots by Peel and clothes by Poole, or was it the other way about? ... Does any one remember the lyric for a wonderful ballad sung by Walter Pidgeon in *From A to Z* at the Prince of Wales Theater in London in 1923, starting "For you were made for me, and I was made for you; I didn't know it till I was three, but when I was four I knew?"

The greatest honor ever bestowed on me from the stage was closing night of *Twentieth Century,* which I had paid to see seventeen times, I was so fetched by it, when Moffat Johnston presented me with the by then worn-to-shreds fur-lined overcoat he had worn throughout the run of the show.... The next most magnificent tribute to me, as a haunter of the playhouses, was when I played a planter with one splendid side in *Poor Uncle Tom,* the Players' Tom show. Both Brooks Atkinson and Percy Hammond neglected Otis Skinner in the leads of their reviews to remark that Beebe was truly magnificent, a latter-day Roscius or the Salvini of the thirties.

The first time I attended a play (what it was is quite forgotten) at the Comédie in Paris I was introduced between the acts in the bar to the then President of France, Gaston Doumergue, and was so fussed by the occasion that I contrived to squirt seltzer, a syphon of which was then in my hand, all over his dress-shirt front. . . . Who remembers that the now tough and rough Humphrey Bogart was one of the handsome gigolos in *The Cradle Snatchers* long ago in the twenties? . . . The most uproarious opening on recent record was of a Hasty Pudding show at Harvard the night the Phoenix Club across the street burned up. The audience to a man deserted the theater and constituted a silk-hatted claque which chanted "Fireman, Save Me Cheeild" as the pompiers attacked the flames. . . . I saw *Jubilee* more times, probably, than any person not connected with the production—twenty-odd. . . . How many times since *Twentieth Century* closed I have seen Dick Maney impersonate himself as directed by the script is incalculable.

The most terrifying evening in the theater was the night of the Rialto cinema disaster in College Street, New Haven. I was the last person to purchase a ticket at the booth and the first one to emerge, carried out by the wave of patrons as the whole premises burst into flame. The lobby of the Taft Hotel across the way was converted into an emergency ward, and a resident bootlegger donated all his stock to the victims while they waited for ambulances.

The last time I saw Noel Coward was at five o'clock in the morning, when he and Libby Holman Reynolds arrived in my apartment and demanded chili con carne,

which had to be procured through the agency of a night
taxi driver from somewhere the other side of Broadway.
. . . I recall the eminent Dick Whorf when he was playing character parts with the late E. E. Clive for the
now defunct Copley Theater stock company in Boston.
The company went up in smoke, ironically enough, because it found a smash hit on its hands. *The Ghost
Train* ran all one season and the next year there were
no subscribers, since the patrons got only one show for
their money instead of the customary change of bill
every month. . . . The celebrated Walter Prichard Eaton,
probably the foremost professor of dramatics in the
land, taught me public speaking in prep school, but in
spite of it I have ever since been the world's worst per-
former when called upon to say a few words in public.
. . . As one of the four stalwarts representing the Greek
Army in the Players' revival of *Troilus and Cressida*,
I dropped my Brooks Costume spear and conked the
late Otis Skinner on the head. After the end of that
scene there were only three stalwarts representing the
Greek Army. . . . The most painstaking production I
have ever seen was *The Green Bay Tree*. . . . Of all
drama reporters I have known the one with the most
fascinating eccentricities was the late H. T. Parker of
the Boston *Evening Transcript*. He wore a red-lined
opera cloak and vintage plug hat, swore like a traffic
cop, and wrote all his copy in longhand so that the
paper had to retain a special compositor who could
decipher his holograph. He used to dine nightly in
Locke-Ober's Winter Place Wine Rooms and knew
more about hock and other German wines than any

A stalwart representing the Greek army

other oenophile of his time, except possibly Dr. Arthur T. Hadley, president of Yale.... The handsomest theater for my money is the Central City Opera House in the Colorado Rockies, eight thousand feet up. When General Grant and Horace Greeley knew it, it had a solid silver floor in the lobby, although this panache of elegance is missing to-day. The ushers still wear Prince Albert coats and riding boots, and opening night each year in Central City is dressier than the Metropolitan Opera.

The most hilarious first night I recall was a few seasons ago in New York when a reviewer for an afternoon paper who had done handsomely by himself at dinner before getting to the opening was taken noisily and indisputably ill in his top hat in a second row aisle seat.

In the ensuing hush a near-by wag remarked audibly: "Why can't these critics wait till they get to their offices before they write their reviews?" ... The most dreadful moment I recall was at the New York opening of Delos Chappell's costly and tasteful production, *Camille,* with Lillian Gish in the title rôle. The undertaking was staged exquisitely, with some of the most wonderful contemporary furniture and costumes on record, and I took Kay Brush to the first night. Toward the close of the final scene, as Miss Gish approached her tragic demise, a fat and dressy fellow directly in front of us urged a blondined and bejeweled tart to her feet and into the aisle, snapped open an opera hat with a resounding plop, and remarked loudly: "Well, I guess she's shot her wad; let's scram for El Morocco!"

The coffee was hot, both ways.

12 *REVERSION TO TYPE*

IT was during one of the coffee and sugar crises which, like the gasoline and rubber crises, beef, tinned-goods, and trouser-cuff crises, have been a familiar part of the pattern of wartime Manhattan. Late one evening, having dined elsewhere, Mrs. Brock Pemberton, accompanied by a party of friends, dropped into El Morocco for a bit of music and refreshment. As was appropriate to the hour, she ordered a glass of cognac and black coffee.

The waiter was desolated, but as she had not eaten on the premises he could not serve her the coffee. The brandy was permissible, but coffee was rationed, a single cup to a diner only.

Mrs. Pemberton was a little miffed and doubted if her demi-tasse would do the war effort any irreparable damage, and Carino, the maître d'hôtel, was sent for.

"You remember prohibition, Carino?" asked Mrs. P. "How we all got used after a while to having cocktails bootlegged to us in a coffee cup? Well, now that times have changed and the liquor is legal and the coffee is not, don't you imagine you could just bootleg me a little black coffee in a cocktail glass?"

13

FORMERLY CLUB

T ARRIERS at the bar at Bleeck's Artists and Writers Restaurant in Fortieth Street, a whole generation of them as New York drinkers go, have been forever turning to one another and remarking that somebody really ought to write a book about the place! It really was worth a book!

Although nobody has ever written the book, Bleeck's is not unknown to beautiful letters and is a standard of currency with newspaper columnists, paragraphers, and sports writers. It achieves frequent magazine mention and has otherwise figured in the more fugitive moments of the muse. For Bleeck's, like all unique things, defies classification and maintains a raffish individualism which baffles all attempts at formalized portraiture. It is a club, a tavern, a public deadfall, an address, an arena fragrant with the souvenirs of mighty contests with bottles, wits, and fists, a repository of immemorial legend, and a monument to the supremacy in the vital life of the town of the whisky bottle and the rotary press.

As solid and respectable in its every visual aspect as any gentleman's club on Murray Hill, Bleeck's is still possessed of a sly and latent atmosphere of hooray. Located on the littoral of Manhattan's Ghetto, the garment district, it has nourished and comforted with its resources the lofty intellects of chief editorial writers and managing editors. Its regulars have ranged from the best minds and most corrupt kidneys of the staff of the immediately adjacent *Herald Tribune* to Crazy Bob Clifford, the Merry Mortician, and on one occasion, Mrs. S. Stanwood Menken, a fashion queen and great lady of dowager proportions. It was before its slightly soiled mahogany that Stanley Walker muttered his immortal aphorism: "Cirrhosis of the liver, the occupational disease of the reporter!" It was in its rear room that Henry George, the big eater, consumed one Christmas day, six entire roast capons, twelve Southdown mutton chops, a four-pound chateaubriand and then, when Bleeck flatly refused to serve him further, shook an angry fist at the management and stamped across the street to the Greek's "where they wouldn't turn a man away hungry on Christmas!"

It was at Bleeck's that Harry McCormack, the demented barkeep, imagined he maintained a complete poultry farm and apiary behind the bar. The premises, in his fancy, were filled with white leghorns and bees in clover, and he was forever scattering imaginary cracked corn to his flock among the duckboards back of the ice bins. He was an excellent barkeep. It was from Bleeck's that Howard Barnes, handsome and scholarly drama reporter of the *Herald Tribune,* disappeared one hot July morning after fifteen Manhattans

and wasn't seen for a fortnight, when he returned to
his duties after a casual exchange of wives.

It hasn't been hard to build Bleeck's into a legend.

From the point of view of an internal decorator, the
Artists and Writers Restaurant (Formerly Club) isn't
such a much. Its heavy mission furniture and fixtures
were designed with an eye to the occasional tantrums
of bemused copy readers and the legerdemain whims
of the late Edward Dean Sullivan, the Lionel Strongfort
of New York reporters of his era. Affixed to the mirrors
are the accustomed array of memorabilia: wireless mes-
sages from Byrd at the South Pole, signed drawings by
Ding and other newspaper artists, opera playbills and
posters for current rallies and causes, photographs of
celebrities, and all the usual museum pieces which
arouse wonder, conversation, and thirst in bars the
world over. Joined a few years ago to such art treasures
as (1) the only oil painting by the late Clare Briggs
believed to be extant; (2) a reconditioned sailfish of
uncertain history; (3) an autographed chromo of
Freddie Bartholomew; (4) the great James Thurber
panel of drawings depicting the progress of the match
game; (5) the cement-filled suit of armor which has
broken many a playfully swung fist—was a fetching
water-color of a red New England barn with a silo to
match. The author of this bijou, which Bleeck accepted
in lieu of a bill outstanding for a considerable quantity
of whisky, had entitled the picture "Waiting For
Thespis" as a humorous commentary on the little summer theater vogue, a movement which was predicated
on the availability of country barns. The canvas was
at once discovered by a pair of bibulous customers, one

of whom was cataloguing the fine points of the place to an out-of-town friend. "This here's a picture about them Fifth Columnists," he was overheard to say. "You find them rats everywhere nowadays. Look at the title: 'Waiting For The Spies'!"

Originally the Artists and Writers (Club) was a speak-easy of notable proportions run by a strangely excitable Hollander named Jack Bleeck. It was Bleeck's heretic notion in those days that only the best booze and most liberal drinks should pass across his bar. Cocktails were seventy-five cents and worth twice as much. It was almost entirely dominated by the staff of the *Herald Tribune,* although a few stylish outlanders like Skipper Williams and the august Charlie Lincoln of the *Times* were always made handsomely welcome. The city editor on duty in an age when Stanley Walker used to head the assignment sheet with the daily entry "Calvin Coolidge: Cover Northampton Situation" (Cal was a contributing columnist at the time) was certain to be able to assemble a fabulous staff of reporters in an emergency simply by calling the bar downstairs. At one time he had his pick of Alva Johnston, Dennis Tylden Lynch, Beverly Smith, Henry Cabot Lodge, Jr., Edward Dean Sullivan, William O. McGeehan, Don Skene, Percy Hammond, Ned McIntosh, John O'Reilly, Ben Robertson, and Herbert Asbury. Some of these luminaries were members of other departments and highly specialized feature writers but all and any were glad to pitch in on city assignments if the occasion demanded.

The front footage of Bleeck's in those days was camouflaged by a fruit-stand under Levantine management, and the bar was in the back room along with the restaurant proper, the men's can, and Harry McCormack's ghostly Plymouth Rocks. At one time in this period the municipal administration, beset by moral wowsers, conducted a campaign against horse betting, and a uniformed policeman was in twenty-four-hour attendance outside the phone booths to listen to all conversations and see to it that no bets were made on the premises. He was not concerned with violation of the liquor laws, which was a Federal affair, and it was long considered the best assignment in the Fourteenth Precinct.

The change from a speakeasy run exclusively for men to a legitimate restaurant open to the wholesale public grieved Bleeck and gave the regular customers a bad turn. It also confused Miss Dorothy Thompson, at the time a starred contributor to the *Tribune's* feature columns, who, one night after her initiation to the wonders of the former poultry rookery, now open to bug-eyed *gobemouches,* told friends that she had been taken to a fabulous place called Jack Bleeck's Formerly Club! Hadn't it said so on the sign outside the door?

Bleeck's has always abounded in the gags, wisecracks, epigrams, and practical buffooneries characteristic of newspapermen, actors, press-agents, and the camp followers of their callings.

One fine noontide during the most bitter years of the Second World War, Robert Paul Anthony (Collapsible) Kelley, so known because of a habit of folding up and going to sleep among the cuspidors without much warning, of the sports staff of the august *Times,* encountered his friend Caswell Adams, of the *Tribune* sports staff, at the bar and paused to pass the time of day. In the course of their chit-chat Kelley had occasion to mention that a common acquaintance of theirs, Richards Vidmer, a former sports writer himself, had just received military advancement, had, in fact been promoted from a captaincy to a majority.

Adams reeled as from a blow, clutched at the bar for support, and smote an anguished palm against his forehead as one receiving, say, the news of a latter-day Flodden. Then, rallying, he took a quick pull at his drink, straightened himself with an obvious effort, and exclaimed determinedly:

"Nevertheless, I *still* think we're going to win!"

The table enclosed in partitions at the entrance to the back room at Bleeck's has, from time immemorial, been reserved for members of the *Tribune* staff at lunchtime and is known as the Press Box. It was at lunch there one day that the writer had the ghoulish satisfaction of taking Howard Barnes at a wager of John L. Gates proportions. It was an era when New York was tearing up all its street-car routes in favor of autobuses, and, knowing his associate for a train enthusiast of vast proportions, Barnes murmured conversationally over the hassenfeffer that he'd just seen the tearing up of the last rail of the old Seventh Avenue street-car system and wasn't it too bad there would never again be any trolley cars in Seventh Avenue!

More technically informed in such matters, the writer was agreeable to five hundred dollars that there would be trolley cars running on tracks in Seventh Avenue next morning, and Barnes, equally persuaded of his own infallibility, took him on with the speed of light. It remained for the writer to point out that the Broadway cars, before turning east into Forty-second

Street, still had to cover a full city block in Seventh past the Times Building in Longacre Square.

"Trapped by a fiend," screamed Barnes, as he reached for his check-book.

Next day he was to recover his losses when a water-main explosion tore up the Broadway cartracks and no trams were routed through for hours. Beebe had said there would be traffic over the rails "the next morning"!

It was from the Press Box, too, that William Harlan Hale, the boy historian, covered the World's Series one year. Hale, a youthful wonder just out of Yale with a couple of learned tomes to his credit, was writing feature copy at the time on the staff of Frank Noyes' Washington *Star,* and, as a variant from scholarly essays on French canon law under the Carolingians, his managing editor thought it might be salutary if he covered a ball-game.

Making merry with a posse of scoundrels from the adjacent editorial rooms, Hale was loath to depart the Press Box for the Polo Grounds and an unacademic midst of shirt-sleeves and pop bottles. He wished it would rain and the game would be called.

It was Bleeck's pleasant whim in summer to ornament the fire escape leading from the rear window of the Artists and Writers with a grass mat, a prop trellis of vines, borrowed from the National Theater hard by, and a couple of brightly painted iron garden chairs. For added realism there was a garden hose, attached and in working order, and bemused patrons sometimes liked to water the stage-set garden in the afternoons.

Within a few moments of Hale's prayer for rain a

deluge suddenly descended in the areaway, splashing against the window-panes and running across the sill in midget Niagaras. The heavens had opened for his accommodation, and, as kind friends were quick to point out, there would never be a ball-game in such a cloud-burst. The downpour increased to simoon proportions, and Hale lingered happily at table. It wasn't until he emerged two hours later to find the sun blazing brightly in Fortieth Street and the pavements as dry as Death Valley that he began to harbor suspicions. Fritz the waiter had been despatched by Hale's impious associates with instructions to play the garden hose against the window from the cellar door and keep it spouting as long as was necessary.

The regulars at Bleeck's have ranged, in recent years, from Ogden Reid, editor and publisher of the *Herald Tribune,* and his editorial janizaries, to waifs and strays from the *New Yorker,* and stage notables such as Noel Coward and Tallulah Bankhead. Jimmy Walker, Jimmy Cagney, Frank Sullivan, John Garland, Owen Davis, Jr., and an assortment of Hollywood celebrities have made it a stamping-ground. Katherine Vincent, the *Tribune's* resident Lady Diana Duff Gordon Cooper, has been for years the undisputed empress of its mahogany. J. P. Morgan, the younger, was an unwitting patron of its fine arts collection in the form of a stuffed sailfish of homeric dimensions caught by his very own hand and snatched for posterity by some *Rod and Gun* editor of forgotten identity. The royal house of Folke Bernadotte of Sweden gloried there and drank deep (and for free) at the time of the historic Folke Bernadotte–Manville nuptials. The episodes attendant to this circumstance are reported to be responsible for the silvering of Bleeck's luxurious mop of hair.

Hardly any social, political, or economic event during the span of its existence has failed to find some echo, some repercussion of its importance at Bleeck's. When the King of Siam visited New York to search out the world's best physicians, his uncle, a lively little prince attired in silk hat and Prince Albert coat, became enamoured of its Gothic premises and spent happy hours, presumably incognito, listening to tall tales from the reporters, press agents, and Broadway characters who crowded his table and screamed, "Otto, a Ballantine's and soda for His Royal Highness!" with fine observance of royal punctilio. When Judge Crater disappeared, headquarters detectives regularly combed the premises for the absentee jurist on the theory that sooner or later, as at the Café de la Paix in Paris, all the world passed through the Artists and Writers.

That major social charade, the Manville–Folke Bernadotte marriage of the glittering twenties staged an olio or so at Bleeck's. It will be recalled that the arrival on these democratic shores of the Count Folke Bernadotte of Visborg, nephew of the King of Sweden, surrounded by a shimmering court entourage, to seek in wedlock the hand of Estelle Manville, heiress of the roofing material family, did not exactly escape the attentions of the homespun American press or the bread-and-cheese people of a simple-mannered land. Seldom, in fact, has there been such tumult and hurrah in the society pages, and if neither of the contracting participants could be listed as strictly members of the old aristocracy, the Bernadotte ascendancy having dated

from Napoleonic times and the Manvilles from an
appreciably later date, the solvency of the entire project
lifted it to a very exalted position in the public mind.

The Count's party, brave with related Bernadottes,
awash with court functionaries, dukes, countesses,
grooms, lackeys, monocle grinders, royal capon basters,
pressers of pants to princes, bursars, ice elephant carvers
for the caviar, colonels, princes, and a few plain Swedes,
was put up by the Manvilles in a state to which it was
quite certainly unaccustomed. State dinners of regal
proportions, morris dancing in the manicured Manville
gardens, *fêtes champêtres,* picnics with Abercrombie
and Fitch overtones, and stately pageantry involving
the Gloria Trumpeters abounded on every hand and
kept the populace in spasms of delight.

And it was during the season of Metropolitan Opera.
Naturally the opera was the only suitable divertissement for royalty, and to the opera the hapless Count
and his suite were escorted night after night by the unsinkable Mrs. Manville. And, equally naturally, the
thirsty and decoration-spangled gentlemen of the court
discovered about Bleeck's, only sixty seconds at a brisk
walk from the parterre boxes. Night after night for two
whole weeks the bar in the back room was jammed, as
soon as the curtain went up on *Carmen* or *The Love of
Three Kings,* with such a glittering array of uniforms,
court costumes, knee breeches, battle ribbons, sunbursts,
single eyeglasses, and fancy manners as the regulars had
never encountered outside a film version of *The Pris-
oner of Zenda.* Naturally the only drink for such fashionable folk was champagne, and they were very thirsty
gentlemen indeed. Also, in those days of illicit guzzling,

vintage wine came at twenty dollars the bottle. The parade of bottles, magnums, and double magnums across the bar resembled the ordered regiments at a French military funeral, but, strangely enough, no cash passed into the till in return.

The answer of course was that the royal party, having been introduced to Bleeck's by a member of the Manville family, imagined themselves in a gentleman's club, an illusion understandably heightened by its exclusively masculine patronage, its subdued décor, and the general absence of all the manifestations they had been given to associate with an American speakeasy. Bleeck, on the other hand, delighted with his handsome and gaudy customers and impressed by their every magnificence of title and appearance, instructed his staff never to even think of mentioning money.

"They're all kings and dukes," he said grandly. "They never think about anything as coarse as money."

And evidently they didn't, for one fine day the wedding took place and the chivalry of Sweden sailed for home, having run up, but not footed, a bill for some eight thousand dollars worth of Clicquot, Moet and Chandon, and Perrier Jouet in assorted years. Bleeck tore his silver locks, muttered about bankruptcy and suicide, and toyed with the idea of window-sills, revolvers, and death under the wheels of the subway cars. Somebody, however, tipped off Ed Manville, who laughed uproariously and promptly forwarded Bleeck a check for the account and no questions asked. It was the merest incidental to the damage done his pocketbook in other directions, but it was a close call for the Mermaid Tavern of the *Tribune*.

"They're all kings and dukes!" Bleeck said grandly

At the time of repeal, one of the qualifications for
licensing establishments like Jack's was the production
of evidence to show that the institution had actually
existed before that time as a bona fide club, so the inmates of the Artists and Writers went to work to fabri-
cate a book of spurious minutes to testify to the essentially private character of the spa. Langdon McCormick,
the stage designer and author of more than a hundred
blood-and-thunder melodramas, was elected president,
Stanley Walker was elected librarian (the only periodical ever subscribed to was the *India State Railways
Magazine*), and Roy Chapman Andrews and Heywood
Broun constituted a billiard committee. There was, of
course, no billiard table, but its exact physical disposition in the middle room occupied endless debate, all of
it fully recorded in the *ex post facto* minutes. Voting of
funds for various humane, patriotic, and scientific enterprises was a constant testimony to the public spirit
of the members. Was the Navy shy a battleship? A suitable sum was immediately voted, and the treasurer,
Harry Staton, the *Tribune's* syndicate manager, instructed to act forthwith. Did old Joe Doax, the printer,
fall down a coal hole and break his neck payday night?
"Defray all expenses of the funeral" was the immediate
fiat of the committee. The sum of one thousand dollars
for the annual clambake and chowder party of the club
appeared regularly in the minutes.

So much fame has attended the rise of the match
game in recent years that the details of this essay of
chance and skill need no more than the barest rehearsal,
but it was in Bleeck's that the match game first saw the
local light of day, whence it spread to Dave Chasen's in

Hollywood and so in the space of a few years embraced in its thrall the whole American continent. Scholars claim to find antecedent traces of the match game in the armies of Cyrus the Elder of Persia, and foreign correspondents of the early twenties remember that it flourished in the Café Bristol at Marseilles at this period. Certainly its first sponsors in Fortieth Street were Don Skene, then master-at-arms of the club, Frank Getty, then sports editor of the United Press, Martin Sommers of the *Daily News,* Vincent Sheean of *Personal History* fame, Allan Reagan, publicist for the State of New York, and Geoffrey Parsons, chief editorial writer of the *Tribune* and a participant who, because of his dignity of office and senatorial mien, is accustomed to play with a set of solid red-gold matches with cabochon ruby heads. Experts who at one time occupied a bad eminence in the lists of the match game comparable to that of the Greek Syndicate at Monte Carlo include Frank Sullivan and Corey Ford, Joel Sayre, Lee Tracy, the late George Buchanan Fife, Fred Wildman, the salesman of rare vintages, and John Ford, the Hollywood director.

The rich vocabulary of the game was probably evolved by John Lardner and Richard Watts, Jr., and includes such terms as "a horse" when a player correctly guesses the aggregate number of matches in the collective hands of the participants. A "horse" is only one leg of a complete game, since winning is predicated on a two-out-of-three basis. The player who leads off a game with an orthodox or conventional number of matches, a mean somewhere between the potential high field and low, is said to make "a Tschaikowsky opening." A turn of hands which reveals all the players holding their maximum possible number of matches, three, is greeted with shouts of "lumber," and a variant on the Tschaikowsky opening is Howard Barnes' scream of "bubkiss" for a conservative guess.

14

"OVERLY INTOXICATED"

ORDINARILY a midst of almost pastoral tranquillity, Bleeck's has occasionally been the scene of stirring encounters and hairbreadth 'scapes. The reverse of Sherman Billingsley's famed Stork Club—where fisticuffs are so frequent that a standard Broadway gag entails saluting its proprietor with the line, "Hey, Sherman, who's fighting at your place tonight?"—the peace is kept with a loaded night-stick behind the bar and is seldom violated.

An exception to this generality was the terrible Watts-Kirkland affair in 1938, when for a few minutes the front room was indistinguishable from a synthesis of the Little Big Horn, the Bridge at Lodi, and the latter phases of the siege of Stalingrad.

The incident was occasioned by Watts' review of a seventh-rate out-house charade waltzed up in the hope of snaring the attentions of the more juvenile-minded theater trade. It was called *Tortilla Flat,* and its dramatizer, already celebrated as an authority on conversational sewage for his version of *Tobacco Road,* was Jack

Kirkland, a hasty fellow who lived to regret his impetuosity and lack of discretion in attacking a reporter in home territory.

The night after Watts' review had brushed aside the masterpiece as unworthy of adult attention, the *Tribune's* drama critic was having dinner with friends in the back room when Kirkland, with blood in his eye, came in the front door uttering banshee screams for revenge and disembowelment, humorously interlarded with references to his "honor" as a playwright. Watts, in the interest of keeping the peace, emerged from the back room and attempted to smooth the ruffled feathers of the Quixote of the cuss-words, whereupon Kirkland took a pass at Watts and knocked off his eyeglasses.

It was a tactical error which might well form the basis for a chapter in any book on military strategy. The first ally to rush to Watts' assistance, as the blinded reporter groped for his glasses, was Arthur Kuhn, foreman of the *Herald Tribune* press room and no fellow to trifle with. Mr. Kuhn's right, augmented in its initial velocity by a heavy Masonic ring, caught Kirkland under the ear and hoisted him across the bar, where he sprawled on the duck boards in a daze until Henry, the senior night barkeep, rapped him smartly over the head with what may or may not have been a baseball bat the business end of which was swathed in sheet lead, and tossed him over the bar again, to the side where customers belong.

By this time Watts had discovered he had more friends than he had ever imagined, all eager to have at his attacker with boots, chairs, bottles, and all and any adjacent blunt instruments. Bleeck, apprized of the massacre by the rebel yells and Ojibwa whoops which filtered back to his table, arrived with what is known in police circles as a sap, shouting as he came: "We don't allow overly intoxicated people here, and no fighting neither," and got in a few slaps before it was apparent that Kirkland had for some time been quite insensible to the attentions he was receiving. The body was booted through the door, just as Howard Barnes, informed of what was toward by a hasty phone call to his desk upstairs, was entering. Fearing that the assassin was escaping the premises, Barnes delivered an admonitory kick in the face and dragged the playwright back again, where the shellacking was repeated, while Bleeck danced around waving his blackjack and announcing that no "overly intoxicated" persons would be served in his saloon.

Kirkland was as good as new a month later.

It was about this time that Watts, an inveterate amateur of Irish whisky and practically nothing else, went on the wagon for some obscure reason. After the passage of a few unhappy days, the hanker, characteristic of all tosspots of any standing, for sweets began to agitate his person and he sneaked, with coat collar up and hat turned down, into a neighboring Schrafft's and boldly commanded a chocolate ice-cream soda. To his surprise and no small dismay, he liked the arrangement and found himself ordering another. When this was consumed he smacked the glass resoundingly down on the soda counter, looked the young man who had served him squarely in the eye and demanded: "Well, what about one on the house?"

An institution incidental to and practically dependent

for its existence on Bleeck's was, until the wars came, a flotilla of taxi cabs of less than dubious automotive origin which stood on the corner cab rank and were known to the initiate and the staff of the *Herald Tribune* as the Vestris Cabs. They were so christened by Don Skene because no board of underwriters would ever have given them clearance papers, and the ancient herdics were likely at any moment to open up at every seam and founder with all hands. Their crews comprised two brothers, Shorty and Isidore, known, for less than no good reason, as Joe, and Irving, known, for every reason in the world as Jumbo. In the old days of the Percy Hammond era the hacks were really fabulous crates, valetudinarian arks with floor space enough to give regimental balls in and jungle thickets of cushions and fringed and tasseled curtains in which a stranger could easily become lost for days without an experienced native guide. Late revelers emerging from the Formerly Club and their home addresses and personal mannerisms were known by the scores to the Vestris drivers. They were familiar with the residence of every newspaperman of account in town, and if the palsied and inanimate were borne to their cabs by Bleeck's waiters there was never any need to search their persons for police cards to know right where to deliver a comatose reporter, editor, or even publisher. They knew the shortest cuts to Great Neck if Gene Fowler was to be ferried home and how to get at a minimum meter fare to the suburban villa of Bill Houghton at Plainfield, New Jersey.

Upon one occasion, when Katherine Vincent was running a series for the fashion page of "What They

Think of the Girls" and enlisting the contributions of such eminentos on feminine attire as George Jean Nathan, Boris Karloff, Billy Conn, and King Vidor, she solicited a mass interview from Irving Cohen, Isidor Aronson, and the brothers Jacob and Charles Kurland, which rocked the town on its heels and caused epic repercussions in the ateliers of Fifth and Madison Avenues.

Another, usually annual, diversion which originated at Bleeck's was a zany devising of Langdon McCormick, the president of the association, and known as the White Horse–Red Headed Girl Contest. It was dreamed up by the distinguished author of *How Hearts Are Broken, Wanted by the Police, When the World Sleeps, Custer's Last Stand,* and *The Millionaire's Revenge* in an unoccupied creative moment, and its progress was reported at column length and with suitable solemnity, usually by John Lardner, in the *Tribune* each spring. McCormick claimed that it was a biological and anthropological fact that there were as many red-haired girls in the world as there were white horses, with the result that books were made at the bar and one Sunday every May the entire clientele would climb into taxis, each under the supervision of an accredited referee, and the boulevards were scoured for these rare collector's items. The amounts involved were prodigious, and feeling among the bettors ran so high that their passions required frequent cooling draughts at every speakeasy along the way. The institution came to an unhappy termination amid bad feeling and near blows when a contingent of white-horse enthusiasts ran into a circus parade, guided—it was claimed by the opposition—by

Beverly Smith, himself of the white-horse faction. There were loud cries of "fraud" and "money back," and nobody could ever again be induced to participate in this sporting event.

For many years a distinguished feature of Bleeck's was a legendary character of Damon Runyon proportions named Don Skene, a sports writer for the Tribune and a wit of considerable fame. He divided his time between the Formerly Club, Sardi's and the upstairs Forty-fifth Street lounge at Frankie and Johnnie's, was reputed never to go to bed at all and maintained a residence in a single room in a theatrical hotel of more or less gaudy repute. One evening Skene was attracted by a commotion in front of the Forty-fourth Street Theater which proved, upon investigation, to be a first night of minor importance where the management had engaged the services of a vast number of police to dress the scene and make it look very big time indeed. The mounted officers were galloping up and down the sidewalk and the foot detail was herding imaginary crowds hither and yon. During his investigation Skene was shoved. He shoved back, bad feeling ensued, and in practically no time he found himself at the nearest precinct station, charged, as he later explained, "with resisting a Shubert opening."

The war had astonishingly few repercussions in Bleeck's. Uniforms, to be sure, put in an appearance, but the place hadn't the appeal to the riotous military on leave of the gaudier puddles in the dim-lit reaches of Times Square a few blocks away.

There was, however, the bright summer noontide of the great Navy invasion when a grizzled commander, his uniform ornamented by innumerable battle and service ribbons, but quite unknown to any habitué of the Formerly Club, made his appearance and put the place to rout. There was no reason to doubt that he had been out all night or had avoided any number of other pleasure domes. He had on a honey, but he was also a man of circumstance and years and there was no refusing his command, given in tones that would have defied gunfire and tempest, of drinks for everyone at his expense. Bleeck's wasn't accustomed to such spacious gestures and its duplicate, by anyone of less commanding presence and station, would have been ignored by the staff. There was no ignoring the commander, however, and his hospitality was shared, if not exactly approved, not once but several times.

At length the old man of the sea was seen to be subsiding. The shouted commands for refreshment became less urgent. His legs took on a quality of the best synthetic rubber and, in a short time, he was enjoying what Milt Gross used to call, in his fables of "Nize Baby," a "dip slip" upon two massive tables which, in his last moments of seagoing resourcefulness, he had pulled together to make a Spartan couch.

What to do? What to do? Nobody was ever allowed to lie around Bleeck's unconscious at any hour of day, let alone in the bright noontide. Nobody seemed willing to take the responsibility of putting him in a cab and the cop on the beat, Pilate-like, washed his hands of all responsibility. It was a matter for the Navy. Summon the shore patrol!

Two nice young men in brassards and nightsticks put in an appearance and shook their heads sadly. Not for them to lay hands on a commander. They had their careers to consider.

In desperation the barkeep on duty phoned the Fourteenth Precinct Station and appealed for help to Captain William Smith. It was a matter of protocol and what was to be done?

In a short time a highly competent lieutenant of New York Police, unaccompanied by any underlings, put in an appearance, partly roused the bottle-scarred veteran and escorted him to a cab. The commander opened a bloodshot and aggressive eye to see who dared lay rude hands on his rank, observed the handsome gold and blue insignia of the lieutenant, closed his eyes and went tranquilly to the waiting hack. Protocol had been observed and he was entirely amenable to reason so long as it was commensurate with his station. The day was saved.

One of Bleeck's most notable patrons, until the great falling out mentioned in the preceding essay, was Henry George, a man of more than ample proportions and capacities and sometime assistant to Fred Hosli, the head house carpenter at the Metropolitan Opera across the street. Mr. Hosli is himself a fellow of no picayune appetites, and his customary evening snack, sent across by a waiter toward the final moments of *Aïda* or *The Bartered Bride,* was a dozen assorted cheese, ham, and chicken sandwiches on rye, confections which made Arnold Reuben's blanket-size arrangements look like the veriest tea-room snacks, and two dozen bottles of iced beer. Thus sustained, Mr. Hosli was able to keep everything under control at the Met until the final curtain, when he would go out to supper.

But Henry George was a true valiant of the stewpots,

a Bayard of the steam tables. Three waiters at the
double were required to serve him the most trifling
collation which might occupy his fancy, and a cold
lunch in mid-August was likely to include in its tale
an entire Kennebeck salmon accompanied by a pail of
hollandaise, three or four loaves of French bread each
the length of a riot stick, a couple of dozen hods of pale
beer, and the entire contents of the French pastry divi-
sion on the service counter.

The legend of Mr. George's phenomenal exploits at
table was received around town, when they made the
public prints, with a certain degree of skepticism by
folk who didn't believe the coefficient of expansion of
the human stomach was practically infinity, so upon one
occasion John O'Reilly, a reporter noted for strict veracity, was assigned by Stanley Walker to keep a tally on
what went into the George face at a given sitting. The
total amounted to the following: six dozen Cotuit oysters, a two-quart tureen of mock turtle soup, a roast of
prime beef weighing just under six pounds, four full-
size steak slabs of cold Virginia ham, a dozen scones
filled with whipped cream, three bottles of claret, eight-
een bottles of beer, and countless sundries in the form
of rolls, butter, radishes, coffee, and sweet oddments.
Mr. George walked from the ring unassisted and asserted before witnesses that he had been a trifle indis-
posed that day and was, therefore, just toying with his
food.

Another favorite, when he shows up in Fortieth
Street, usually with what he happily refers to as a cinders
case bound for Arlington Cemetery, is Bob Clifford,
the Newport undertaker, known to the clientele at the

Artists and Writers as Crazy Cliff, the Merry Mortician. Cliff, who has buried the Newport ornaments of the worlds of aristocracy, fashion, and wealth, and is entirely aware of the abysmal gulfs that separate these categories of society, possesses the added enchantment of looking like an undertaker out of Cruikshank and has most of the ghoulish attributes of his calling. He carries a pocket rule and is forever sneaking up behind drinkers at the bar, who are for the moment happily unaware of mortality and the worm; applying a folding ruler to their persons, he announces: "Ha! A good six-foot-six job. I'd suggest bronze handles! Something costly but in perfect taste!"

"Death, it's hilarious!" he is accustomed to shout with graveyard overtones, weaving among the palsied drinkers at the bar.

Cliff, according to the saga and his own gaudy report, achieved his fair repute as the first gravedigger of the Providence Plantations by securing the assignment to bury one of the more notable Vanderbilts, a commission which practically put him in a position to announce his services as purveyor to royalty. The aging notable in this case was accustomed, each morning before breakfast, to slide by means of a smoothly constructed chute, from his bedroom window into the ocean cove adjacent to his villa, a gentle incline of several hundred yards across the lawns and gardens. During his easy progress toward the refreshing deeps he read his morning mail, tossing idle and inconsequential stuff to the left and invitations to be answered in the affirmative, tradesmen's accounts to be settled, and matters of import to the right, where they were retrieved by secretaries and underlings and dealt with according to their arbitrary classification. Being apprized that the Vanderbilt scion was failing in health, Cliff posted a boy with a pair of binoculars on an adjacent knoll commanding this morning pageantry, to report on the state of being of his prospective customer.

Sure enough, one morning the urchin arrived breathless and pregnant with tidings of mighty import. Mr. V. was having unfinished-business trouble: he was carrying part of his mail, unopened, into the water with him!

"I knew he was cooling then and there," related Cliff, "so I walked in on the family and gave them a very special bargain offer in advance, and got the business just like that."

"It was a mighty fine cinders case, too," Cliff says in tones of positively unguent satisfaction. "Real tufted satin, gold handles, everything the very best! That's what comes of being forward looking. You've got to be in my business!"

An occasional pilgrim to the Fortieth Street oasis was Selmer Fougner, wine and food reporter for the *Sun*, a gusty and inflammatory personage who not only could consume homeric quantities of fodder and sluicings but also could talk endlessly about them and, indeed, made himself a very nice thing out of his syndicated columns. He even went so far as to found a sort of gastronomic academy known as Les Amis d'Escoffier, one of the strictest regulations of whose charter was that there were positively to be no speeches made at its œnophilic congresses. At least none by any one but Fougner, who was accustomed at these Byzantine repasts to rise to his

feet during the dessert and deliver impassioned orations
on the fabrication of le canard sauvage à la presse Tour
D'Argent, or the virtues of the Pinod grape as exempli-
fied in the '29 clarets, masterpieces of rhetoric of which
Dan Webster would have been proud, and which lasted
as long as there was a bottle of vintage cognac convenient to Selmer's hand.

He was, however, democratic in his drinking prac-
tices and, after sniffing and swallowing the rarest vintages which Fred Wildman or other of the town's leading wine merchants could provide, was known to race
for Bleeck's and start in on the real work of the evening
with a tumbler of straight Wilkens Family on the bar
in front of him, pausing in its consumption only to
extol in Warren G. Harding periods the quintessential
magnificence of the 1920 champagnes.

Fougner at length came to a fine end and died filled
with foie gras and truffles and leaking Romanee Conti
at every joint, and Ray Ahearn, the barkeep at Bleeck's,
voiced the common opinion that when, in fields Elysian,
Ganymede paused behind his place with a chalice of
vintage ambrosia, Selmer would promptly send him
back to the service bar for a bottle of squareface gin.

Another of the gallery of Bleeck's notables and a
character right out of Gene Fowler at that, was Skipper
Williams, ship's news reporter for the *Times* and dean
of all the cutter and barge office boys in the lush days
when transatlantic travel was filled with news and excitements and the water-front assignment was not taken
over by the United States Navy. His real name was
Walter Williams, but Skipper he lived and Skipper he
died, and almost three decades of voyagers knew his

cockney accent, his fantastic anecdotes, and the dicer hat which was the hallmark of portly coming and going in the Lower Harbor. He was at heart a rogue, a liar in the grand manner, a figure of importance, and a person at whom folk looked twice. In his invariable bowler, wing collar, and umbrella, he even contrived to impart a sort of elephantine grandeur to the hazardous business of climbing a foot-wide board from the customs boat into the half-ports of an arriving liner off Quarantine in a choppy sea. His barroom mendacities were on a heroic scale, his ribbing of young reporters a legend, his talent for snaring free meals, drinks, shaves, and shoe-shines on incoming liners a technic that would have engaged the admiration of François Villon or the other great free-lunch artists of history. He occasionally wrote long chronicles about a fabulous figment of his imagi-nation—Marmaduke M. Mizzle, the Mincing Lane car-away seed merchant—and his beer-parlor anecdotes and autobiographical souvenirs, some of them authentic, others possessed of all the legitimacy of a Confederate shinplaster, could hold his audiences by the day, or as long as they were solvent enough to foot the bar check.

Just as the regular hangers-on in most New York saloons of consequence include a posse of horse-race bookies and tipsters and often enough a sort of profes-sional fixer for motor licenses and minor police arbitra-tions, so some of them have a built-in resident jeweler, usually known as Jeweler Joe, who purveys modest items of bijouterie to the regulars at presumably reduced rates. Sometimes, like a character known as Pepino, whose headquarters is at John Perona's table in the expensive vistas of El Morocco, they are legitimate gem vendors

able to undersell the Fifth Avenue retailers because they
maintain no office and hence no overhead. Sometimes
they are authentic hot ice merchants, fences, and distrib-
utors of valuables of uncertain antecedents. For years
Bleeck's had a Jeweler Joe who would turn up anything
from a Van Cleef and Arpel's platinum cigarette case to
a fifteen-dollar wedding ring at half price, given a little
notice. He did a thriving trade among the regulars,
and it was popularly expected, when news of his death
in a Saranac retreat came to hand, that he would leave
a huge estate. In the end Bleeck had to pay for his funeral. He had lost all his profits to the horse bet makers
who had been giving him daily tips at the bar for years.

A frontier legend practically intact from the era of
Pawnee Bill and Buffalo Bill Cody occasionally descended on the terrified palefaces among the cuspidors
in the form of Ned Alvord, the old-time carnival press-
agent, a celebrity in every saloon in North America from
the Hurry Back in Salt Lake and the Crystal Bar in
Nevada City to the Switch Key in Fort Worth and the
Palace in San Francisco. Alvord's claims to immortality
are many and varied, but his outstanding achievements
are in the spheres of attire and profanity. His accustomed costume when he appears at Bleeck's, usually on
the arm of Dick Maney, is a seersucker cutaway with
trousers to match, a pearl-gray top hat of Mississippi
River gambler proportions, Texas boots and spurs, and
an assortment of diamonds profusely and tastefully scattered about his person. Discovering him once in the bar
at the Astor wearing a broad diamond-studded stom-
acher as a sort of panache to the rest of his wardrobe,
Whitney Bolton suggested to Lee Shubert that he be

retained instanter and billed for a nation-wide tour as the Yankee Escudero, after the Spanish dancer then enjoying a popular vogue.

Next to his clothes Alvord's vocabulary has been for years the wonder and glory of North Platte, Teluride, and the Texas Panhandle, and it is reported that he once made a bet with Gene Fowler as to who could clear out the premises of a restaurant faster by merely raising his voice in ordinary conversation. Alvord won hands down in the Hollywood Brown Derby, where, in five minutes flat, he had the frightened patrons in the street, leaving him and Fowler seated in lonely and dubious glory, for all the world like Cataline in the Roman senate. It is reliably reported that printers dived through the composing-room windows on the occasion that he attempted to secure proof of a four-column ad in a Tokyo paper when on tour with a nonesuch called *A Night in Paris.* This was the confection, a dreary routine of Bronx grandmothers in fly-blown spangles, which Alvord shoved down the reluctant gullets of three continents, billing it as "a stupendous carnival of sex and abandon, imported at vast expense directly from the Folies Bergère of Paris. Not since the dawn of time has there been convoked such a congress of beauty," To illustrate and guarantee these promises Alvord plastered Shanghai, Sydney, Madrid, Mexico City, Cape Town, and Antofagasta with three-sheets depicting the charms of a quite undraped nymph—from the rear. The caption under it read: "At eight o'clock to-night she will turn around!"

Never tethered by facts, Alvord and Maney, abetted by Amon Carter, plastered the entire state of Texas with propaganda advertising the fascinations of Billy Rose's first Aquacade on the occasion of the Texas Centennial celebration at Fort Worth. They evoked a Babylonish vocabulary, hitherto unencountered by the guileless cowhands and oil drillers, wherein every B-girl, late of the Wabash gin parlors in Chicago, became "the favorite of the late Emir of Afghanistan, a houri of legendary voluptuousness snared from the seraglio of the Sultan to ravish your senses with her exotic fascinations." When Dallas, the traditional rival of Fort Worth in all things civic, put on a somewhat more abated exposition of its own, with less accent on gunfire, whisky slings, and the fatal charms of harem voluptuaries, Maney and Alvord dreamed up a slogan which illustrated every billboard from Aransas Pass to Nogales and from El Paso to Brownsville: "First go to Dallas for culture, then come to Fort Worth for fun!"

John Murray Anderson, who has been involved in a number of dramatic skirmishes with Alvord, is fond of recalling that on another occasion the coiner of bagnio superlatives had distributed a blizzard of posters throughout the Middle West heralding the wonders of a dog and pony show by depicting a number of conventionally naked ladies in an assortment of September Morn poses. A great cry of horror and outrage went up from the local women's clubs, and the proprietor of the carnival rushed to his agent to demand an explanation and possible repairs for a bad situation.

"What the hell did you expect me to show them?" countered Alvord. "You know they wouldn't pay a nickel to see John the Baptist!"

On another occasion Alvord tried to induce Anderson

to help him with the projected tour of a girl show in Japan.

"Whatever do you want to go back to Japan for?" asked Anderson. "You know the time you were there you didn't even see Fuji!"

"I know," quivered Alvord, "but I want to be the only person alive who has never seen Fuji twice!"

"I don't want to be heard," is a favorite aphorism with Alvord, whose unamplified whisper blasts plate-glass windows from their moorings. "I always want to be overheard!"

During the blue days and fair of what Westbrook Pegler likes to call the era of wonderful nonsense, a frequent ornament of the Mermaid Tavern of the Tenderloin was Hector Fuller, herald of the City of New York, scroll reader to Mayor James J. Walker, and majordomo of City Hall in an age when civic receptions and municipal barn raisings achieved a magnificence unknown since the fabled extravagances of the Field of the Cloth of Gold. A stately and plausible fellow, Fuller, with his silk hat, cutaway, and resonant oratory often enough defective in content but never orally, was vastly admired at a time when it was a lean week that lower Broadway didn't toss telephone books and cartons of lily cups out of the windows at triumphant channel swimmers or returning round-the-world fliers. Fuller was handsome, seventy, always thirsty, and could recite more English verse than any one in Bleeck's except Dick Maney, and bemused reporters, weary of precinct stations and sidewalk suicides, would listen by the hour, pausing only to refresh the minstrel's glass, while he recited Swinburne, Dowson, Dobson, and

Tennyson with unfailing memory and persuasive enunciation. Plain-clothes men from Center Street and whiskered gaffers from the rim of the copy desk would maintain a deathly hush while the stanzas of "Locksley Hall," "The Triumph of Time," and "Cynara" were forthcoming as long as there was a highball handy.

Fuller dreamed up the scroll which, in that halcyon era, was presented by the city, through his hands, to distinguished visitors. It was when Captain George Fried was returning to the country after one of his heroic sea rescues that the Mayor, Rodman Wanamaker, and Grover A. Whalen were sitting around the Stork Club, then located uptown near Seventh Avenue, and wondering what to do about it, that the scroll came into being. Then and there on the back of a menu Fuller devised the text of the testimonial, which, suitable in gold leaf and hand lettering, became the standard Manhattan award of chivalry or swimming prowess.

"It cost twenty-one hundred dollars," said Fuller later, "but what the hell! New York is rich!"

He composed other scrolls at Bleeck's, and reporters, press-agents, and actors in rehearsal at near-by playhouses contributed their bits to their ornate and flowery mannerisms.

Sometimes, after a prolonged session at Bleeck's with a Roget's *Thesaurus* handy, Fuller would give his plug hat a brush, step into a municipal limousine, and head for city hall and oratorical disaster. He got names and titles wrong and once publicly saluted Premier Pierre Laval as "Prime Minister Paul Claudel." On another occasion he hailed Queen Marie of Romania as "Your Imperial Highness," a lapse of protocol which passed practically unremarked in the happy confusion of the moment.

After Mayor Walker met his Wellington in the person of Judge Samuel Seabury, and after the departure for high office in Washington of his other patron, William H. Woodin of the American Car and Foundry Company, times grew lean for Fuller. Scrolls were no longer in municipal requisition, and a usurper held the throne at City Hall. Fuller never batted an eye or turned a hair. He paid his last bar check at Bleeck's one winter afternoon and went home and turned on the gas. His friends last saw him, distinguished even if silent, at Campbell's Funeral Home, his ledger-ruled morning trousers creased to a knife edge and in his lapel a single gardenia cabled to him from his friend Mayor Walker, an exile in England.

Although Wilson and Addison Mizner, so far at least as the record shows, were unknown to Bleeck's mahogany, the establishment had its veterans of the Yukon and gold-rush days, as every proper bar should have, in the persons of Fred Wilson, long the senior night bartender, and Jack Hines, the monocled minstrel of Rincon Hill in San Francisco. Both of them retained fragrant souvenirs of the spacious days of Tex Rickard and Jack London in Alaska and the age when the Poodle Dog, the Barbary Coast, and the overlords of the Southern Pacific flourished wickedly in St. Francis' town and vast numbers of men of bounce commuted with the seasons between a pre-fire Palace in Market Street and the beach at Nome.

Hines, a graying but undaunted sportsman and a pal of Messmore Kendall, Major Edward Bowes, Arnold

Genthe, and other San Franciscans of later Manhattan residence, had been a banjo player in Rex Beach's minstrels in the Yukon days, a gay dog in the lush decades on Nob and Russian Hills after the celebrated conflagration and was, in the early forties, acting as master of ceremonies in a night club supervised in the cellarage of the Brevoort Hotel on Fifth Avenue by Joe Zelli. Jaunty, waxed of mustaches, and sporting a rimless single eyeglass, Hines used to drop into Bleeck's for an occasional refresher and maybe a tip on something at Belmont. His constant plea for excusing himself was that he had a rehearsal of some gay-nineties songs with his accompanist, a lady with whom, it was reported, he was accustomed to tour the hot spots of Broadway when in funds. The lady, while doubtless a paradigm of gentility, culture, virtue, and beauty, would have small truck with insolvent escorts.

One happy Saturday Hines became involved in a series of match games and horse plays and was missing appointments with the accompanist every half-hour. Finally, through a process of elimination, she caught up with him on Bleeck's pay phone.

"I'm desolated, my dear," Jack's courtly accents were heard echoing from the booth by fascinated listeners, "but I am in a low stews and have fallen among thieves!"

The answer was not precisely audible at the bar, but the tones in which it shook the spavined telephone cubicle were undeniably hortatory and emphatic in the suggestion that he get the hell out of her life, accompaniments and all, forever.

What Hines didn't bother to explain was that, while it was quite true that he had fallen among thieves, he had immediately associated himself with them and was even at that moment $250 ahead in horses and match winnings.

Overly intoxicated patrons are discouraged

Fred Wilson was a barkeep of what has traditionally been known as the "old school." A silver-haired mixer of modulated manners and quiet accents, his lore of Alaska wisdom was illimitable, and his drinks, based on the formulas favored by poke-laden sourdoughs, possessed an authority unknown in prohibition Broadway.

A failing memory clouded his last years, through which he was carried to a gentle end by Bleeck.

But of all the occasional inmates of the Fortieth Street zoo during the entire decade of the thirties, the most glittering, zany, and legend-shrouded was Charles Stanley Sackett, a manager of de luxe uptown hotels, a fabled raconteur, and a leering exquisite whose entry into almost any bar in Manhattan was greeted with happy howls of "Here comes Uncle Stanley!" and a great and universal setting up of drinks. Stanley was only infrequently in funds, save, of course, for the time he inherited ten thousand dollars from somewhere or other and spent it in a week, but so gaudy was his personality and so ingratiating his stories that he was welcome in circles that embraced grand duchesses and truck-drivers, policemen, English lords, brewmasters, and cattle millionaires.

Sackett was, in turn, manager, managing director, renting agent, or whatnot of a variety of hotels in New York and on the Pacific coast. He was the super-front man of such posh hostelries as the Lombardy, Élysée, Vanderbilt, and Madison, and later, for a brief but undeniably gala interlude, managing director of the Palace in San Francisco. His tail-coats, of which he possessed literally scores as contrasted to a single street suit, his hand-kissing, and his lordly commanding of supposedly gratis magnums of Perrier Jouet which might later be found unobtrusively but profitably lurking in a guest's bill—a technic perfected by Rosa Lewis in her Cavendish Hotel in London—endeared him to patrons and managements alike, and under the flowering Ascot tie and urbanity of approach, he knew at a glance most of the skippers, bad check artists, swindlers, and other public enemies of the hotel business in two continents.

"Why shouldn't I know them?" he used to say. "They're all of them my best friends out of working hours!"

Uncle Stanley's undeniable weakness was going on toots. Not just one- or two-day binges which ended with remorse, Bromo-Seltzer, and a chastened return to duty, but big, vital three- and four-week screamers conceived on an epic scale and accomplished with an éclat which usually found him in the Bahamas, Mexico City, or Los Angeles, whence he was with difficulty retrieved and reinstated in office by kind friends.

Upon one occasion, when he was at the Madison, Uncle Stan had a great falling out with the proprietors, resigned with a suitable flourish, and arrived at Bleeck's with a mound of Vuiton luggage, suit-cases, hat-boxes, valises, Gladstones, and impedimenta enough for a concert singer on tour, and announced grandly that he was through with the hotel business forever and was sailing for England at midnight.

In point of fact, he had his passage in his pocket, and it was apparent that some of his more valuable household possessions had gone to the flea market and that he had also visited Simpson, the refined loan agent, on the way downtown. In effect, he was flush, merry, and in a mood to command wine. By the middle evening word of this expansive farewell-forever party had circulated, and thirsty friends and even mere acquaintances had come to bid Stan a fond bon voyage. The queue reached through the doors and out into the street, and, as midnight approached, Stan was hoisted into a taxi, his bag-

gage was tossed in after him, and directions were given
to convey him to his pier in the North River.

"Don't any one come with me, please, boys," he
pleaded. "I can't stand good-bys!"

The next morning the international traveler awoke,
still in his dinner-clothes and on a berth in what was
undoubtedly the stateroom of a steamship. He rang
weakly for assistance and restoratives and was only
mildly surprised when a large and amiable Negro in
a white jacket answered his summons.

"Cunard changed to colored stewards, eh!" remarked
Uncle Stanley. "Well, that's nice, although I must say
I hadn't heard of it!"

"This ain't no Cunarder, sir," beamed the darky.
"This am the Norfolk boat and we're there now. You
better get up and dressed, sir."

There were times in Stan's life when the Norfolk
boat was only very vaguely distinguishable from the
Berengaria!

The foregoing are, of course, only a few highlights
and low woodwind noises from a Manhattan saga which,
while not, perhaps, possessed of historic greatness, is still
representative of the spirit of an era and a locale. Many
verses and chapters must survive, like the Homeric material, only by word of mouth, such as the occasion when
a prominent Boston industrialist, on the town for the
marriage of his son, was inadvertently locked in the
men's washroom at closing hour and, having lost his
spectacles down the drain and not being entirely sure
of where he was, was unable to find his way to the front
door to summon help: he remained closeted with himself until next morning at eleven, when John Gallagher,

the day barman, opened up and released him. Much, too, that was robust and of arresting importance at the moment loses its fragrance with time and becomes unsuited to printed record.

Helen Hayes has always maintained that Bleeck's doesn't exist at all; that it is simply an Indian rope trick and the figment of somebody's disordered imagination. Escorted there one evening by her husband, Charlie MacArthur, of *Front Page* fame, she discovered that life in Fortieth Street was every bit as demented as had been represented to her, worse perhaps. At one table Nunnally Johnson, Darryl Zanuck's most expensive vicar, was beating his third wife, whom he had married that afternoon, over the head with a silver handled umbrella, a wedding present from Fred Wildman, screaming the while: "You'll never have my autograph, woman!" Dick Maney with his hair in his eyes like an English sheep dog, was matching passages from *Troilus and Cressida* with Dr. Henry Rowell of Johns Hopkins, also a notable recitationist. Crazy Cliff, the merry mortician, was measuring folk for imaginary coffins with his undertaker's measuring tape, and Bleeck himself was shaking an admonitory finger at two terrified and entirely blameless sailors who had wandered in under the impression they could enjoy a quiet glass of beer and telling them that no overly intoxicated people were allowed on the premises. Bleeck always takes it for granted that all members of the armed forces are stewed on general principle. Miss Hayes was, understandably, persuaded that the worst she had heard wasn't a patch on the real thing and that Hallowe'en in the madhouse would be a rest cure by comparison.

But much of doing and undoing has passed before its mirrors. Great news stories have been broached there, celebrated canards plotted, the destruction of the mighty and the elevation of clowns to high places has been set in motion over its crystal beakers. It was at its back table that most of Stanley Walker's *Mrs. Astor's Horse* was conceived and written; it was from Bleeck's that Gene Fowler set out, loaded with canned goods and copy paper, for a winter of solitary labors on *The Great Mouthpiece* on Fire Island, a winter frighteningly destructive to the morale of his only neighbors, the members of the Coast Guard; it was here that Joel Sayre in his reporter's days, Nunnally Johnson, and Alva Johnston have splintered the furniture in their comings and goings and that Harry Staton started the revived vogue for "The Man on the Flying Trapeze" which marked a musical period in the barbershops of 1935. Dexter Fellowes, with his plaid overcoat and silver-headed stick, first stopped in there to announce the annual descent on the town of the Circus and there Tallulah Bankhead was known to stand on her hands while singing "God Bless America." George Buchanan Fife, the dandy reporter of the *World,* used to sport his square bowler and come-to-Jesus collar for the admiration of younger reporters; Dudley Field Malone turned up one day, after years of absence from New York, to celebrate his portrayal in *Mission to Moscow* of Winston Churchill. There was, and still exists, a regular *Herald Tribune* luncheon clique including Howard Davis, the business manager, Geoffrey Parsons, the chief editorial writer, Howard Barnes, the drama reporter, and William Morris Houghton of the editorial page staff, which always appeared at twelve-thirty, their waistcoats festooned with heavy gold Albert watch-chains, a symbol at once of substance and of Victorian respectability. It was from Bleeck's that Ben Robertson, laden with silk stockings, chocolate bars, and perfumery for Joseph Evans and other correspondents in London left for the Clipper to take him in his last flight to Portugal. They found Ben's body after the fatal crash in the Tagus but no trace of the goods for which he was messenger. There was, too, Minnie, the house cat, who was beloved of stars from the Opera across the street when Bleeck's was originally situated at Fortieth and Seventh Avenue. She knew Scotti, Caruso, Lawrence Tibbett, and Mario Chamlee intimately and liked to lap up a refreshing Martini herself if it were placed for her in a saucer on the bar. She knew William J. Fallon when he was a rising young lawyer. She even made friends with Albert Payson Terhune, a professional lover of dogs, and she was on the best of terms with Joe Cook, the comedian, Winsor McCay, the cartoonist, Clare Briggs, and W. O. McGeehan.

Now Minnie is with the ages, along with many of her friends, a player in an allegory of lost causes, but still participant in a sort of bright and raffish immortality, along with all the boys before the bar and singing "Clementine" in the back room.

15

STEIN SONG

HE manner of life of Manhattan in the early thirties will, of course, one of these days be a matter of absorbing interest to social archæologists, and some of their finest monograph material they will find in the flounces and flurries, the tumults and confusions which accompanied the more or less liberal arts of the era. The audiences which attended ballet performances are, alone, worthy of intensive scholarly research. Such manifestations as the art of Salvador Dali and other practitioners of the absurd, either more and less fraudulent, present illimitable vistas of potentiality for the connoisseur of the hilarious. No practitioner of what passed for "modernist" technic in her sphere of activity survived longer before being rolled under the wave of the world than Miss Gertrude Stein. Her strictly runcible prose was the precisely identifiable forerunner of what later became known as double talk on Broadway a full two decades earlier in the Paris of Elliot Paul, the Deux Magots, framboise at Lipp's, noonday cocktails in the Ritz, Coté Cambon, and the appearance of the first volumes of Frank Harris's *My Life and Loves* at Sylvia Beach's bookshop in the Rue de l'Odéon.

In the middle thirties Miss Stein wrote and caused to be uttered and produced an opera which, played by an all-Negro cast in transparent attire, was the artistic success foolish of the season. It opened at Hartford and came to New York, and, before or since, there has never been anything quite like it, an actual testimonial to the existence of a just and merciful God.

In the form of elderly dowagers with lavender-dyed hair, willowy youths in ponderous jewelry from the art galleries of Fifty-seventh Street, a troup of Negro players from Immense Thespians, Inc., casting agency, the script of Miss Stein's opera with a score by Virgil Thomson, the New Art in upper case letters overwhelmed Hartford in the winter of 1934 in a manner that would have made Mr. Byron's fold-bound Assyrians the merest amateurs of catastrophe.

It was an invasion that Tamerlane would have applauded and a subsequent massacre of the bourgeoise proprieties that would have given the late Oscar Wilde the vapors, and if Billy Rose could have been present on opening night he would have wheeled his Casino de Paree off to Kane's Warehouse as a dreary and dismal burlesque. For, as a Bedlamite flag-raising, it took all sweepstakes, Calcutta, Irish Hospitals and Canadian Veterans', hands down. Armed with a jargon which included the entire vocabulary of a modernist technic, the participants put the nutmeg capital to the torch with volcanoes of blazing indiscretions. Snipers armed with thirty-six-inch cigarette tubes took pot-shots at the

petrified citizenry fleeing through South Main and
Asylum Streets, and when the din and carnage subsided
sufficiently to allow the stretcher-bearers to reach the
scene, the field was strewn with murdered unities, de-
capitated conventions, smashed top hats, and Moet and
Chandon magnums. Two days later the only sound was
the distant firing of gossip guerrillas knocking off a few
surviving reputations with epigrammatical fowling
pieces.

Since the Whisky Rebellion and the Harvard butter
riots there has never been anything like it, and until
the heavens fall or Miss Stein makes sense there will
never be anything like it again. By Rolls-Royce, by airplane, by Pullman compartment, and, for all we know,
by specially designed Cartier pogo sticks, the smart art
enthusiasts of the countryside converged on Hartford
for the dress rehearsal. The production was under the
auspices of the Friends and Enemies of Modern Music,
of which the agreeable and distinguished A. Everett
Austin, Jr. was the moving spirit. Mr. Austin was also
chief executive of the Hartford Art Museum, of which
the Avery Auditorium is a unit.

Four Saints in Three Acts opened against a rival
attraction in the form of a Connecticut bartender's convention and bartender's ball, and hotel rooms were at a
premium. At least one important New York delegation.
which included the Count Roussy de Sales and Harry
Bull of *Town and Country,* were forced to put up at
what amounted to a Turkish bath hotel, a circumstance
which threw them, they asserted, into a suitable trance
from which to contemplate the cellophane harmonies of
the new opera. Miss Phillis Byrne and Samuel Chot-

zinoff had better luck, while the *Herald Tribune's* Gertrude Stein reporter was tendered bed and breakfast by the hospitable Bill Foote, of Hartford *Courant* fame.

The lobby of the Avery Memorial is thoughtfully provided with two grand staircases leading down to it, so that two grand entries, engaging, of course, the attentions of two posses of cameramen, can be made at once. It was for this reason that the entire assembly of chivalry selected one of them as its own particular gangway and an innocent society reporter was badly crushed. It was the bystanders who suffered most throughout the evening. The curtain was conveniently late, and everybody had a chance to make at least two grand entries, and some of the more enterprising got around as many as five times. Mr. Bull, who takes his own pictures, used up a reel of film on Carl Van Vechten alone. Muriel Draper was runner-up for attention. A large group of real Hartford folk who had been to the James T. Sobeys' for cocktails slipped unobtrusively in by the disused stairway, and the curtain went up to the accompaniment of thunderous applause.

The real show, however, was at the intermissions. For the first five minutes conversation was as guarded as that in a Pullman smoker in wartime. Nobody wanted to admit he didn't know what it was all about and take a chance that he was talking to Miss Stein's publisher, but as soon as the Messrs. Kirk Askew and Julien Levy had burst into unabashed tears because they "didn't know anything so beautiful could be done in America," the hysteria was on and a blizzard of superlatives was in progress. Little groups let down their back hair and cried quietly in corners for beauty. Sandy Calder, who was the only person present who thought tweeds were indicated for the occasion, said he would just as soon have cried for beauty, too, but that it would dilute his punch. There seemed for a time to be danger of a catastrophe that would make the Johnstown flood look like nothing at all until Miss Jean Sears, Henry Cabot Lodge's sister-in-law, laughed right out loud and said she was going to look for her lifebelt, when every one laughed, too, and felt all right again.

The second intermission was even more gala. Every one promenaded, and the photographers had a field day. They snapped the orange whiskers of Professor Henry Hitchcock of Wesleyan University and the lavender hair of Gertrude Newell; they surprised Eddie Warburg, who was the youngest member of the board of the Metropolitan, in full anecdotal career, and Josiah Marvel, of the Springfield Museum of Fine Arts, beaming amiably. They detonated bulbs over Kenneth Pendar, of Sioux Falls, South Dakota, and the Knoedler Galleries, John Henry Hammond, of Henry Hammond, Inc., Broadway producers of *Little Ol' Boy*. Alan Priest of the Metropolitan Museum, the Count Roussy de Sales, and, of course, Mr. Austin, and they snapped plateless shutters at a great many lesser celebrities just so there would be no hard feeling. It would be hard to imagine that anybody had a dull time of it, unless perhaps it was the young man who committed the trifling solecism of wearing a pair of pale gray trousers with dinner linen and jacket and who didn't get pictured at all, not even from the waist up.

Altogether it was as gala a field day as Hartford is likely to see these many moons. After the amazingly

"A rose is a rose is a rose is a rose"

abrupt last curtain there was an uproar that would have brought the police from Central Station in a jiffy if Mr. Austin hadn't warned them in advance. "You know what these Gertrude Stein fans are," he had said to the captain on duty. There were curtain calls by the score. Professor Hitchcock of Wesleyan smashed his opera hat with gay abandon and howled for Mr. Thomson. Mr. Thomson made a bow. Professor Hitchcock tore open his collar and shouted for Mr. Austin. Mr. Austin made a bow to Bedlam and a sea of fluttering handkerchiefs. It was a good thing for the proprieties there weren't many more people for Professor Hitchcock to shout for. After that the cast dropped in exhaustion on the stage, and every one went to an enormous party at Mr. Austin's house, not forgetting to take his program, which contained a portrait of Mr. Thomson by Miss Stein beginning "Yes ally yes as ally" and called it a night.

16

HOME ECONOMICS

THIS is a chronicle of household economy which is certain to be of assistance to all bachelors and hotel dwellers, and which concerns itself with the time I became savagely determined to have asparagus in January and not pay Colony prices for it either. Disaster in the match game at the hands of Stanley Walker and other dinner-jacketed bandits at Bleeck's had reduced my resources to approximately those of Mike Romanoff in the era when he used to sleep in Dan Moriarty's coal bin.

Across from my hotel, in the window of the Madison Grocery, was a jar of asparagus stalks, a good triple portion of those rather thinnish, dark-green sprouts, the kind that gave promise of actually tasting like asparagus, and the price was eighty-five cents. This was something less than thirty cents an order, I figured cannily, and I'll bet my hotel gets $2.50 for a stingy half-dozen stalks at this time of year. I would show them. So I purchased the asparagus.

The circumstance that I had never coped with any

aspect of kitchen life more complex than the compounding of a Martini and that my apartment had no resources for cooking didn't in any way abate my enthusiasm for high living at low cost. The management would feel pretty sick, I argued, if it knew that I was saving approximately $6.65 by eating a triple order of asparagus for practically free. The only apparent way to heat the stuff, in the absence of a kitchenette and cooking equipment, was to put it into a bathtub filled with scalding water and leave the tap running gently to keep the heat constant. So I ordered the house dinner, price $2, and sat down to my crabmeat followed by genuine pre-rubber-rationing chicken, feeling myself a veritable Hetty Green of the stewpots.

The time came when I was to put one over on the management through the agency of my forethought and careful buying, and I went to the bathroom to retrieve my asparagus. It was apparent at once that the room had been converted into a sort of steam bath. The atmosphere had seeped through into the adjacent dressing-room and been eagerly absorbed by a dozen starched evening shirts on the shelf, and, as I entered, a yard-square piece of ceiling disengaged itself from the archi·tectural economy of the building and struck me briskly on the head. These contretemps, however, I viewed as strictly incidental to the main project at hand of saving money on my restaurant bill.

I contrived to scald myself severely up to the elbow reaching for the jar at the bottom of the bathtub. The water looked so clear from standing that I momentarily forgot it was straight from the boiler and achieved a good second-degree burn which kept me in pain for two

I found I could save $6.65

full days and eventually ended by peeling all the skin from my forearm.

When the water was at long last drained off and the asparagus emerged like something at a gastronomic Scapa Flow, it was discovered that nowhere in my non-housekeeping apartment was there any sort of gadget with which to pry the top from a mason jar, and it was necessary to tip a hallboy two bits to bring one from the bar. I attacked the jar vigorously, only slightly impeded by an arm swathed in amateur bandages and anti-burn grease.

There was a hideous cracking sound. Asparagus, scalding vegetable juice, and fragments of glass exploded across the landscape, smearing a pile of fresh linen with green sediment, while the miniature grappling iron which is required to disembowel tins and pots carved a neat and surgically artistic furrow across my left wrist. Since Gettysburg there hasn't been so much blood. I reached for the telephone to summon the house doctor to sew me up, dripping gore on bedspread, brocaded chairs, and carpet. The room was a shambles. So was I.

The itemized cost sheet of my domestic gesture of economy follows:

To Madison Grocery: 1 Jar Asparagus . . . . $ .85
" Doctor for Home Visit Requiring Four Stitches   20.00
" Doctor for Subsequent Visit and Removal of
      Stitches 10.00
" Hotel for New Bathroom Ceiling 15.00
" Laundry: Twelve Starched Evening Shirts .   4.80
" Bellhop for Can Opener 25
" Dry Cleaning Bedspread 2.00
" Dry Cleaning Business Suit 1.00
" Night Maid for Renovating Premises . . . 2.00
                    Total . . . $55.90

That's the trouble with these luxury hotels. You pay too damn much for incidentals.

17

ON FAME

Nowhere in the world is it as nearly impossible as it is in New York to avoid arbitrary classification or to escape a label once it has been associated with one's name in the public prints. Once the reporters, paragraphers, and columnists have dreamed up a character for some one, he may as well make up his mind to live up to and with it, for it will follow him to the grave, and his obituary will use it as the pattern of his life story, no matter how imaginary or how little representative of his true person it may be. For some unidentified reason, variety in a person's character or versatility is unthinkable to the editorial mind, and once a president of the United States has participated in a hog-calling contest, he will be known to posterity as the hog-calling chief executive, no matter what else his achievements.

A prime example comes to mind in the person of the late Mrs. S. Stanwood Menken, a lady of multiple charms and graces and a vast resource of wit, who, because of her association with the Beaux Arts Balls of fragrant memory, became inescapably associated in the public mind with exotic costumes, fancy raiment, and towering headdresses. As a matter of record, save for a single event every year, an event which, at that, occupied but a few hours of her time, she was as conservatively got out as Whistler's Mother and probably spent less attention, time, or money on her clothes than the vast majority of her acquaintances. But because of her one happy fling at the Beaux Arts she came to represent in the public mind the last word in costly attire this side of Mrs. Harrison Williams.

Newspaper caption writers love a tag, and so does what passes with a titter as the literate public. It simplifies everything.

Take, for another example in the realm of feminine fashion, Mrs. Orson Munn, who is pictured in the public prints as, perhaps, not quite right in the head because of her eccentric taste in bonnets. That she has a variety of interests and a private life of her own, quite dissociated from the lunatic devisings of Lilly Daché, never enters anybody's mind.

Long after he is gathered to his fathers it will be recalled that James Hazen Hyde distrusted the devisings of a mechanical age and preferred to drive through the streets of New York in the horse rigs to which his youth was accustomed. It will be quite forgotten that his activities as a cut-up of the boulevards led to the Equitable Life Assurance scandals which elevated Charles Evans Hughes to the office of governor of the State of New York and later the Supreme Court of the United States.

In much the same manner, Crosby Gaige is going to

A tag simplifies everything

be known to posterity as the man who never stops eating, a result of his association with the Wine and Food Society and other tongs of tosspots and eatalls, although he is also one of the best living printers, an amateur gardener of note, and a sometime theatrical producer and wolf of Broadway. Clara Bell Walsh is almost entirely known for her elevated position as one of the "thirty-nine widows of the Plaza" and is famous for her address rather as a considerable landholder in the Blue Grass region of Lexington and the widow of Julius Walsh who made himself a comfortable fortune selling Royal typewriters.

It is entirely probable that Harold Ross will, one of these days, be less celebrated as editor of the *New Yorker* than as the possessor of a mop of hair which caused one wag to describe his appearance as that of a "dishonest Abe Lincoln." Al Smith's brown bowler, Kelcey Allen's fondness for giving away mechanical gadgets on opening nights at the theater, Brock Pemberton's savage sarcasm, and Gilbert Miller's penchant for calling royalty by their first names, all of them trivialia and no more than the hallmarks of personality, not its essence, incline to become better publicized than the true characters and achievements of the celebrities with which they are associated.

The author of the deathless word paintings of which this essay is an integral part is a classic example of the old adage of "Give a gay dog a name ..." A fellow of notably retiring habit and self-effacing mien, he was once trapped by professional associates in a something less than formal saloon, which he had unthinkingly entered, attired in morning clothes and accessories en route to divine services or some other function requiring broadcloth and Ascot ties. He was promptly hailed by Walter Winchell and other scoundrels as the Berry Wall of reporters, a Richard Harding Davis of the night clubs, a dude among the legmen, and a penny-a-liner of vast and effulgent sartorial resources. Photographers possessed of low animal cunning contrived to apprehend him, when professional duties took him to gaudy midnight precincts, as one with exquisite associations and given to the upholstered carnalities of the bon ton. It became necessary for him to lay in a stock of tail-coats, Inverness cloaks, and collapsible top hats to live up to the legend, and as time passed it was impossible for him to identify himself at his bank unless he was wearing court attire complete with orders and a dress sword. He was invested in the public imagining with as many sets of cabochon emerald evening studs as Tommy Manville had wives.

It was, of course, all profitable stuff as it turned out and was seized upon by commercialists and exploiters for promotion schemes not altogether unworthy of thrifty attention. But it all goes to prove that once you are tagged in New York the tag becomes more important than yourself.

18

THE MAYORS OF THE PALACE

IT can hardly be said that the mantle of Cesar Ritz, greatest host and restaurateur of all time, ever descended on any American hotel man, although perhaps the late Albert Keller, who worked for and with the Ritz organization for many years, shared much of his distinction. Foreign hotel keeping and restaurant management have always been a solemn, stately, and even pompous calling. Royalty and magnificence laid a heavy mortmain on the business, and such famed American hosts of the last generation as George Boldt, of the Waldorf, and Simeon Ford, of the Grand Union, would have little or none of it.

The leading hotel men, restaurateurs, and club managers of the American scene to-day are almost all gay and witty scoundrels. "Only men of the lowest moral character can hope to become successful in the hotel business," says Ernie Byfield, and he should know. This naturally doesn't apply to the back-office men and credit managers, but when one encounters such authentic entertainment geniuses as Alfred Barton, the late George

Lamaze, Stanley Sackett, René Black, or Byfield himself, he never expects the frock coats, platitudinous formalities, and dead-pan deference of the Continental tradition. Without excepton they are laughers, gag artists, and gorgeous persons. Behind them are the resources of gold plate, powdered footmen, celebrated chefs, crimson carpets, and the upholsteries of grandeur, but their front is uniformly one of airy and casual magnificence.

Even before Ben Hecht and Charlie MacArthur made him immortal in *The Front Page*, Ernie Byfield was a Chicago instituton and one of the ranking hotel men of the generation. Ernie himself says there has, at one time or another, been a movement on foot to tear him down for parking space, but he's still around. The old Sherman House was owned by his father. It was built just after the Chicago fire, but looked as though it had been built before, and its architecture derived from the era when hotels advertised the modernity of their rooms if there were windows in them. The Sherman boasted, somewhere in its complex internal economy, one of the country's first night restaurants with entertainment, called the College Inn, and young Ernie was all for putting the legend "War Is Hell" on all the hotel's key tags, but Papa Byfield frowned on such levity and made him cashier. This taught the old gentleman something of a lesson, as they had to engage four extra auditors to count the postage stamps every day at close of business.

The College Inn and Ernie became national legends together. The place was one of the first widely touted hangouts of stage and literary folk, a sort of Early Silurian Jack and Charlie's combined with Fefe's Monte

Carlo. Its inmates included the Dolly Sisters, Fanny Brice, Al Jolson, Will Rogers, the Astaires, and a juvenile Ray Bolger, whenever they hit Chicago. It was there that John Barrymore used to rendezvous with Lotta Faust during his first stage appearance as a juvenile. Patrons, before the days of high-pressure publicity and the rise of professional social celebrities, were bewildered and resentful of entertainment programs which went through stages of Ruth Etting, Kate Smith, Ted Healy and Maurice and Walton, but suddenly the College Inn blossomed as Chicago's top-notch night spot, when Ben Bernie introduced his theatrical nights in the early thirties and from that day to this no theater person, screen star, or celebrity of importance has passed through Chicago without making obeisance in some form to Ernie, the Sherman, or the Ambassador Hotels.

The first Ambassador was opened in 1920 on the west side of State Street and became Chicago's Algonquin during the town's golden age of gashouse literature. Charlot's Revue constituted one of the first invasions of the Ambassador, with Bea Lillie, Gertrude Lawrence, and Jack Donahue among the assembled barbarians. That was the year that Charlie MacArthur attempted to steal one of the elevators for his New York apartment but was unable to work it out of its shaft after several hours of experimenting. After the hotel had been refurnished and redecorated it was opened to what Ernie calls with a guffaw the general public.

Ernie's recollections are legion: a compound of montage and palimpsest, including Chaliapin drinking two flasks of Chianti and a bottle of Anisette nightly and telling stories of Russian moujiks in his own tongue to

Gregory Ratoff and Judith Anderson; a dinner party at which a then unknown Claudette Colbert soundly snooted Jeanne Eagels and Louis Wolheim; Dorothy Parker and MacArthur meeting unexpectedly in the lobby after their first romance; Bob Benchley first encountering pineapple juice when it was newly introduced, and sending to room service for a pineapple squeezer; Ethel Barrymore being presented with two bottles of imperfectly processed tomato juice, which later exploded, and phoning Byfield in hysterics that her bathroom was running with blood; the assorted lunacies and whimsies of all the Armours, Swifts, Fields, and Cudahys, and Sidney Franklin, the Brooklyn bullfighter, flying into a towering rage when Will Mahoney screamed "Moo" at him.

Ernie's current and probably most glittering of triumphs is, of course, the Ambassador's Pump Room, and it is the management of this platinum pavilion of pishposh which has rounded out his credo that, in addition to being possessed of a naturally low mind, a hotel man must be a synthesis of opposites: a greeter and gladhander one minute and a bouncer the next, a gourmet and wine-bibber on occasion and an ascetic when executive functions demand it, an expert in the arrangement of flowers and the disposition of garbage, a purchasing agent and a salesman, a happy receiving teller and a wary casher of bank drafts, an amateur of swing music and an enforcer of nocturnal quietude, a connoisseur of fine arts and a practical plumber, and familiar with the symbols of life and death from accouchement to embalming.

The Pump Room is, as everyone knows by now, the

ultimate word in mid-continental chic and a filling-station for glamour, social rowdydow, and magnificent food, half-way, more or less, between the Colony in Sixty-first Street and the Palace in San Francisco. It is a dull lunch hour when you can't find Dwight Fiske, Averell Harriman, Eddy Duchin, Chicago's own Peter Moon, Gertrude Lawrence, the current Mrs. Potter Palmer, *Cosmopolitan's* Frances Whiting, Ethel Barrymore, Clifton Webb, and a hard-riding troop of cameramen and reporters doing a double scurry among the rolling tables of salmon in aspic and wheel-barrows filled with iced wines. Gertrude Lawrence, as a matter of record, has a table permanently reserved for her, whether she's in town or not, with a gold-framed portrait of herself in the center.

The motif of the Pump Room is mobility. Everything is on wheels. A great deal of it, too, is in flames. There are vast mounds of fresh fruits packed in glaciers of shaved ice: on wheels. The hors d'œuvres are as wonderfully regimented as West Pointers on the table: on wheels. The cold soups, notably a vichyssoise for which the Ambassador is world celebrated, are nested in their silver caldrons in the ice beds: on wheels. The desserts, pastries, and, dominant over all other rolling resources, the champagnes are rolled to the table of the delighted patron: on wheels.

On the least provocation or none at all, Byfield admires to produce fire and smoke. A buff of the wine bins, neither Vulcan nor Prometheus nor even Mayor Fiorello La Guardia was ever consumed with such a passion for blazing dishes. At stated intervals, although nobody has commanded their service, platoons of kneebreeched servitors race around the perimeter of the Pump Room waving sabers on which are skewered flaming cutlets of veal and other inflammable viands in the hope of inciting the frenzied spectators to further gustatory excesses. Approached on the subject of this pyromaniacal display, Byfield once told the author: "The customers seem to like it, and it doesn't hurt the food very much!"

In the course of a recent transcontinental hejira to the Palace in San Francisco, Dwight Fiske, the author, and Charles Myron Clegg, Jr., U. S. N. R., contrived to scurry up among them three orders of crabmeat crêpes Louise, blazing mightily, a roast pheasant afire from stem to stern with cognac, an order of cherries jubilee, one of peaches flambé, a ditto of crêpes Suzette, and three beakers of café diable, making a grand total of ten table conflagrations, any one of them calculated to strike terror to the heart of a fire commissioner. All that was lacking was Mrs. O'Leary's cow to lend a pyrotechnic panache to the carnival of combustibles.

Byfield has come by his fair fame not alone as a Caliph of Caviar—he once carried on the Pump Room menu a "golden" sturgeon roe at twenty dollars an ounce—but also as a wag. Once when George Bradshaw, a fictioneer familiar to readers of the *Saturday Evening Post,* was in transit between Washington and San Francisco on government business and was trying to get a quick snooze between planes in one of the Ambassador apartments, he was recurrently awakened by what seemed to be a congress of cross and argumentative sparrows on the ledge outside his window. "For gossake," he screamed into the telephone at Byfield, "if I've got to be kept awake by your damn Chicago birds, why don't you, in a swell dump like this, at least have thrushes?" Half an hour later Bradshaw detected more melodious chirpings from the balcony and discovered there a cage of ten canaries. A later note from Ernie supplemented the replacement. "Sorry," it read, "but these are wartimes and we're all out of thrushes. Lily Pons ate the last of them in a pie yesterday. You'll have to rough it on canaries!"

Upon another occasion, when visiting New York to see Katharine Cornell, Judith Anderson, and Ruth Gordon participating together in a production of *The Three Sisters* at the Ethel Barrymore Theater, Byfield sent the following post-performance wire to Kay Cornell:

Miss Katharine Cornell,
I love you madly and send my undying devotion to you alone. Only you could arouse such admiration in my heart. From one whose fidelity is yours and yours alone of all the women in the world.

> (signed)　Ernest Byfield
> Copy to Miss Judith Anderson
> Copy to Miss Ruth Gordon

Camille Duplieux, the maître d'hôtel and "Frenchy" to the intimate great, used to be a room-service waiter until one day Kitty Byfield said to Ernie: "We have the duckiest floor waiter named Camille. He always tucks me in mornings after he brings my breakfast," and next day Frenchy had charge of the Pump Room. Another now vanished but not forgotten character of the Ambassador was Clark, a house detective highly esteemed by Ernie but loathed by Charlie MacArthur. Charlie maintained that the only illicit couple ever unearthed by Clark were, in fact, legitimately married, and when he married Helen Hayes he sent Byfield a wire: "Would have spent our wedding trip with you but were afraid of Clark."

Like the Colony, Jack and Charlie's, the Palace, Antoine's in New Orleans, and Perino's in Los Angeles, the Pump Room has become one of the great glamour restaurants of the land. As such it is naturally not without its detractors. One prominent Hollywood Communist, after spending a good part of his $5,000-a-week salary rolling around among the vintage champagnes, recently wrote in the guest-book: "There isn't anything wrong with the Pump Room that a good revolution wouldn't fix." Whereupon his escorte, frightened out of her pretty wits by such temerity, left the table and flew from the premises, as Ernie remarked from his table, "like one unpossessed."

Another of the adroit majordomos whose sense of showmanship has, in a more modest but nonetheless staggeringly successful manner, brought celebrity and success to his tumult parlors is Sherman Billingsley of Manhattan's Stork Club, an institution born not to blush quite unseen, and often, by reason of the number of major battles and fistic engagements staged in its purlieus, mistaken as an East Side branch of Madison Square Garden.

It has been contended that behind the urbanity and savoir faire, in the most exacting sense of the phrase, of Billingsley, there lies the coaching and imaginative spadework of Steve Hannagan, a super-press-agent and exploiter whose genius has been credited with lending glamour to a number of vast undertakings ranging from the Union Pacific Railroad's Sun Valley to the Vanderbilt Cup Races. Be that as it may, no act, however well rehearsed, could completely account for Billingsley's vast competence as proprietor of the most widely touted night club in America.

Aside from the excellence of its food, a circumstance often underrated by even the most knowing diners-out in New York, and the name bands which tootle current airs to the customers, the Stork is a monument to flattery judiciously distributed and always with the best possible eye for effect. Billingsley's sense of social and promotional values hardly ever makes a mistake. He distributes free orchids and other costly corsages, magnums of champagne, Cartier clips and match-boxes, dollar cigars, and other glittering largesse to customers who will most appreciate it and will talk about it most afterward. He has an uncanny sense of who is important and why, and major generals and leading industrialists may not rate a nod from the master, where an enlisted soldier or small-town couple on Manhattan holiday are greeted with the noisy installation of extra tables, the ceremonial presentation of corsages from Schling the florist, and the always acceptable uncorking of a bottle of spectacular if essentially meretricious wine.

The answer, of course, is that the major general can hardly afford to be a playboy in the puddles and that his position, like that of royalty, is a lonely one and without many friends. He would, in all probability, admire vastly to be singing sentimental ballads with the top sergeants, but the obsolete and nowadays entirely comical usages of the military art and mystery prevent it. And no amount of flattery can impress the industrial magnate, since he knows what it's all about anyway and will return to spend his money if the place pleases his wife whether or not he is snowed under a blizzard of expensive flowers. The enlisted soldier, on the other hand, may very well be an old and accustomed patron with a social and financial background which would effectually prevent his association with commissioned persons save in line of duty, and who, in any event, is young, impressionable, and pleased with the flattery of attention. He has friends by the yard and his boast of "Sherman's a friend of mine, you just ask for Sherman," is a recommendation which is not within the gift of princes or advertising agencies. In the same way the small-town boy and girl on holiday will talk about the Stork when they return home as no debutante ever carried on about her presentation at the Court of St. James's.

The tally of purveyors to the de luxe tastes of the affluent through the various devices of showmanship as synthesized with food, drink, amusement, and luxury ways of life in general, might, if space were available, include many more majordomos of note than can be listed here. It would embrace, for instance, Mrs. Eric Blore, steward of Charlie Farrell's incomparable Racquet Club at Palm Springs, where, with the possible exception of the Palace Hotel in San Francisco, the most distinguished food and drink in all California once obtained and may to this very moment. Ma Blore, when members of the Racquet wished to entertain in a handsome manner, was usually given carte blanche by Adolphe Menjou, Rudy Vallee, or whonot, and could

turn out, in the middle of the California desert, meals
starting with caviar as big as pearl shirt-studs and running through grilled Mexican quail and strawberry
soufflé that would pop the eyes of a first-string restaurateur in Paris in the old days.

Such a tally would not omit Colonel Jack Bradley of
Palm Beach, who understood the value of a glittering,
pint-size restaurant as an adjunct to the most celebrated
of American parlors of chance. Only there, so far as the
writer knows, was there achieved a twenty-five dollar
cover charge, an item on the bill for which guests received the accustomed linen, eating tools, and bread
and butter, plus a microscopic vase of flowers.

In many ways Bradley's casino, in the time of its
fullest flowering, was one of the most spectacular gambling establishments in the world, since every aspect of
its décor and conduct was a study in understatement.
Its physical plant was devoid of the florid overtones associated in the general mind with high play and wealthy
clientele. Its atmosphere was subdued to a point where
it approximated a vestry meeting, and only the names
of its patrons and the sums of money nightly played
across its tables were an index to its true character.

The existence of Bradley's was known to thousands
of near-by residents, none of whom ever passed its
closely guarded doors, for no citizen of Florida might
ever be admitted to play in the house either as a member of the club, by the name of which the establishment
was known, or as a guest, a rule as rigidly adhered to as
that which prohibits the Monegasques from entering
the old-world casino at Monte Carlo. Another regulation at Bradley's required that one must be at least

twenty-five years old before he or she become a member of the club, for Bradley was a businessman and would do business only with persons old enough to be responsible. Formal clothes were obligatory after six.

No one ever heard of any one being cheated at Bradley's. The house took a percentage of the winnings, but the thrill was all the more enjoyable when one won. There was never a scene at the club, and Bradley's word was as good as his bond. He was known upon occasion to give back to a "piker" all his losses rather than have anything disagreeable happen.

Membership at Bradley's was about as difficult to obtain as admission to a high-grade New York speakeasy. An introduction by two members was sufficient for admission if the social and financial standing of the prospective customer was apparently good, but casual loungers and non-playing visitors were not welcome, and the sums at stake were no encouragement to the presence of persons of merely moderate means.

Probably no casino in the world was more discreetly managed than Bradley's. The knowledge that any scandal or disturbance on the premises or rumors of dishonest or irregular play would inevitably bring to a close its highly illegal existence served to guarantee the good and, indeed, unimpeached reputation of the house. Its cool white corridors with their green carpets, its palm-furnished lounges and perfectly appointed restaurant where four persons might dine for little more than one hundred dollars off fresh caviar and pompano, graylegged grouse from the Scotch moors and out-of-season asparagus, were all invested with an air of simple refinement and well-bred acceptance of the amenities of social

existence. The servants of the house partook of an un-
obtrusive efficiency, while the score or more of detectives on the premises were indistinguishable in clothes
or manner from the guests themselves.

Three games, baccarat, hazard, and roulette with the
standard, double zero American wheel, were played at
Bradley's. The salle de baccarat was presided over by
a suave French croupier wearing a single eyeglass, who
was brought over from a Continental casino every season, while the two large rooms of the house were devoted to hazard, played with dice and a mechanical boot,
and roulette, the king of all games of chance. It was at
the roulette table that the greatest sums changed hands
when play was high in the small hours of the morning
and the lords of the world's industries and finance were
playing maximums with oblong five hundred dollar
chips stacked in tottering piles before them on the green
cloth of the table wings. It was at such a table in the
back room at Bradley's where only men might play,
that an industrial overlord, the president of one of the
world's greatest motor-car manufactories, dropped a
quarter of a million dollars during an evening's play
and remarked casually, as his last chips were raked in
by the croupier, that he was out of pocket money for
the night, but that he would be back as soon as the
bank opened next day. He returned, as he had promised,
and in two nights' play had won back all he had lost
and a substantial sum in addition.

At variance with the custom at continental casinos,
the players at Bradley's bought their chips directly from
the croupier at the table they intended to patronize instead of from a cashier in the main entrance foyer of

the establishment. The bank notes were slipped into a slit in the top of a steel cash box in front of the croupier, and this box was removed every half-hour to the house vaults where its contents were removed and counted. When a player wished to depart from the table, his chips, if he had any, were bought back by a floor cashier who was summoned by the croupier and who purchased the unplayed chips with currency of large denominations which he carried in his coat pocket. The standard unit of currency at Bradley's was the century note. Notes for five hundred and one thousand were almost as frequently on the table, but anything below a twenty dollar bill was regarded as something of a curiosity.

Bradley's profits have been estimated at between a million and a million and a half dollars a year, and as the average profit to the bank from the three games played in this establishment was about 2 per cent of the total sums wagered, it may be seen that considerable money passed over his green-topped tables every season. And there are few men in the world who could amass money at this fabulous rate and still maintain the reputation for honesty and the squarest sort of shooting that was Bradley's greatest asset.

Nor should the record omit the name of the leading gambler of Houston, Texas, a personage of note in the 'thirties named Jakie (the last name long escapes memory) whose house of chance and personality for years provided pleasure and hilarity to the well-oiled gentry.

Jakie ran a house said to be above reproach in its conduct, and the tycoons of the Humble Oil Company and other vast enterprises of the region assembled there

nightly, but the green tables and shining bird-cages
were less of an attraction than Jakie himself. The proprietor was possessed of a hanker to be a social fellow
and associate himself with the regional nobs, a circumstance which, combined with his gasworks background,
truck-driver conversations, and rough-and-ready person,
was not without its hilarious aspects. Jakie was no Berry
Wall, but he essayed a stylish exterior, with the result
that he unfailingly sported the wrong raiment at any
given time. Did his country club customers turn up for
the evening in sports clothes after a day of golf or riding,
Jakie appeared in a parody of full evening attire. But
did the customers arrive from a formal occasion at the
homes of Weiss or Blaffer, complete in stiff linen and
broadcloth, Jake was sure to turn up in a snow-white
golf suit.

At one time Jakie's authority as overlord of Houston's
underworld was momentarily challenged by an upstart
dice tosser from Galveston who had the misfortune to
be under a Federal indictment for manslaughter. The
new-comer set up a roulette den and made a bid for
Jakie's clientele, but Jakie, secure in his established
prestige, was in no way worried or upset.

"That son of a bitch can't never get nowhere in these
parts," he remarked, "on account of him bein' a moi-
derer! The bastard is ruint social, see?"

Perhaps more than any other big-time operator in the
truffle and plover's egg market, René Black, director of
all the Waldorf-Astoria resturants, is the outstanding
contemporary practitioner of the precepts of Brillat-
Savarin on the American scene. Black, who once washed

dishes in a Nevada mining-camp after a pay streak he was following had run out—albeit at gold-miner's wages of twenty-five dollars a day—is an exquisite among restaurateurs and known to thousands of world travelers, not only for his accomplishments as a maître d'hôtel but also as a tootler on the French horn.

Asked by the writer for an outline of the most elaborate dinner he ever imagined, Black unearthed the following record of two meals he evolved a few years since at his own restaurant in Coronado, one of them for Walter Dupuys of the celebrated French family of cognac kings.

The first course was to be an *hors de concours* presentation of hors d'œuvres, consisting of five playing cards made out of food and so identical with real cards that they caused astonishment, thus winning the first *étape*, so to say. There was a skilful presentation of shellfish on rocks, made of gelatin, with tiny clams, mussels, crabs, crawfish, oysters simulating their natural habitat. The juices of each, instead of being presented in sauce bowls, were offered in their natural shells, and all was imbedded in ice. Served with this was a dry Chablis, Château bottled of 1906 Montrachet. There was a small éclair-looking roll stuffed with Virginia Ham Mousse cooked in port wine, and pâté de foie gras in amber jelly in tiny tartelettes; Deviled midget tomatoes stuffed with small filets of anchovy; Turtle fins in ruby jelly; pigmy artichokes with caper dressing; Pineapple trussed up as a porcupine; shredded tuna in crisp cassolettes. Tiny rolls in the form of a mushroom cake with sturgeon butter. Original wooden barrels with the inscription of the house of caviar of St. Petersburg and the houses they purvey; Roots of Fennel à la Grecque; Russian wheat cakes; aiguillettes of Smoked Eel. Filet of sturgeon with sour cream and evaporated horseradish. Tiny cigarettes of reduced puree of wild mushrooms.

This particular type of hors d'œuvre never has been repeated except in the house of Ponyatovsky in Russia. An ensemble of harp, flute, two violins, and guitar, accompanied by Venetian songs of gaiety, accentuating poetically the hors d'œuvre to the tune of a thousand dollars.

The table properly cleared and the residue put aside so that no waste should occur, a potage made its glorious entry in marmites of sea-gull gray china, in which Consommé Ursuline was presented, same being a very fine broth made of duckling bones, Madeira wine, and the juice of beets, with fine julienne of celery and tiny dumplings of duck meat and hardboiled eggs cut in small dice. Béchamel sauce was served in separate containers. To further accentuate the appreciation of this famous classic consommé, there was a guitar solo by Guido Stefano, the *Malaguena* by Moskowsky.

Golden trout escorted by claws of crayfish, known in gastronomic annals as "La Truite à la Gentilhomme" was the next dish. Crawfish is placed on mousse of shad roe, the trout boned and stuffed with wild rice and spinach to maintain its form, melted butter and nantua sauce, made from the carapace of crawfish, served with it. Also a tiny potato prepared à la Palestrina, stuffed with smelts, and its peculiar manner of cooking without water and a soupçon of white wine, laurel leaves, and rock salt, then mixed with butter. This has appeared on tables such as those of the Aga Khan, King Edward VII, and the Maharajah Kopotallah, whose households had the good fortune to possess culinary masters to follow the good teachings of Carême. The Song of the Pearl Fishers was rendered by Constantino accompanied by a full orchestra and scenery.

Quails cooked in the ashes of clay were served with hot

almond sauce, copied from the Chinese. The guests did not use finger bowls, but there was a little vignette telling them that the Chinese washed their faces and hands. Nor were carved toothpicks presented. The almond sauce was a purée of small hazelnut-size giblets cooked in Madeira wine and served as an escort.

There was Filet of Beef from a prize steer completely buried in charcoal, seared outside and the center very rare. It was cut in very thin slices with the full contents of the meat flavor. Very few cooks have followed this particular secret. Even the French Academy has abandoned the word *bavir* which is the method of roasting a filet in that manner.

Escarole Salad in which the oil plays the important part, completely masked in order to close the pores, then the vinegar prepared with salt, pinch of dry mustard and black pepper sprinkled over all and delicately caressed in order to preserve its crispness. Asparagus was cooked in its own water, its succulence and fragrance of such crispness and spongency that the convives remarked as to its particular type of cultivation and soil. The *Götterdämmerung* was the musical accompaniment of this pièce de resistance, showing the similarity of cuisine to music.

Pistachio Bombe, known as "Verlaine," in molds forming an aurora, the molds being made by the chef, who shows his versatility as a sculptor as well as a master of cookery. Turkish delights and Brazilian coffee, quite bitter to the contrast of the super-sweet Turkish friandises; strawberries and pears of Meran presented as fresh fruit course, the strawberries representing a Swiss mountain with the Benedictine monks' safety station, roads made out of nougat, stems covered with snow made from cream of tartar and fine sugar. Over four hundred baskets of strawberries were used. All the residue was sent to the hospital, the birds to the orphanage and parochial schools.

The wines consisted of Bordeau, Château Lafitte Grand Vin 1893, Liqueurs San Franciscan, and Louis Philippe Brandy 1834. Grand Chartreuse and Benedictine.

The setting of the room was made by Rosa, the scenarist of the Metropolitan Opera, depicting scenes of sunrise and sunset with appropriate landscaping in perspective. A space of three feet was taken from the walls, and wires carried to the ceiling covered with moss and flowers. Behind this setting, four thousand canaries were kept in the dark, and when the lights were turned on, they started to chirp and sing to the accompaniment of Italian singers and Hawaiian singers alternating; the sounds appeared to come from a distance.

Another very interesting menu was for twenty guests, when a fine dinner was served in Coronado. There were Oysters with Chablis, Green Turtle Soup with Amontillado Sherry, Filet of English Sole Normande with Neirstein Hock, Poulard Soufflé Vladimir, Saddle of Lamb à la Broche, Haricots Verts, Pommes Voisin, Guisler Champagne extra dry 1900, Jambon d'York au Champagne, Château Mouton Rothschild 1893; Bombe Africaine, Friandises Croute de Merluches, Mocha, Grand Vin et Liqueurs.

In composing the menu, each dish had its doctrine. In their origin and its ramifications are hundreds of applicable names with their raison d'être. Most people are gourmands, but one is a gourmet when one is an artist or a poet. Taste is a very delicate sense, like eyesight or hearing. To lack taste is to miss an exquisite faculty like discerning great books, paintings, or even perfumes. One must also be a floral artist of vision, besides having legible and characteristic handwriting, a sketch artist, too, and creative in composition of dishes—which it has been my pleasure to introduce to many a patron, such as Foie Gras à la Talleyrand, Les Crêpes au Foie Gras, Consommé Pauvre Moine, Brook

Trout Chevalière, Lamb Chops Petit Duc, Hearts of Artichoke St. Michel, Mushrooms au Foie Gras, Russian Pancakes of Crabmeat, Gateau Czarina, Virginia Ham with sugared eggs, Strawberries Victor Hugo, Pineapple Ninon, and many other dainty entrées which one never tired to ask for at the moment when gourmandise bites the palate.

19

THE CAVIAR CALIPHS

O F the latter-day mayors of the palace, whose palmy days have lasted almost up to now and may be expected to resume when the dust settles, Alfred Barton, sometime manager of Montauk Manor on Long Island, sometime courier to Woodrow Wilson, and most recently manager of Miami Beach's very costly, very chic, and very overpowering Surf Club, is incomparably the most imaginative. A cony catcher in the grand manner and a fellow of infinite resource, Mr. Barton throughout the thirties made the routs and pageantry at the Surf a model to which Cecil B. De Mille was reported to have despatched spies for notes on his own representations of the Fall of Babylon. The widget manufacturers of the Middle West footed the bills for these super fandangos, and the costumes, sound effects, and Nubian slaves were supplied by Alfred I. Barton.

Barton, a fantastic wag to whom his own occupation of shearing the carbureter kings and gasket caliphs was the essence of life, is possessed of the invaluable asset of unfolding panoramas of potential pageantry to a customer, vistas that would cause Haroun-al-Rashid to wince and would give pause to Lucullus himself, without cracking a smile, and himself trading a measure in the most lunatic sarabands without allowing the other participants to apprehend that he is, in fact, waving a bladder with all the regal gestures of a wand of office.

The Surf Club, before it became an airdrome for the armed forces of the land, was one of the high-pressure pleasure promenades of the post-Teapot Dome era, a physical plant with an internal operating economy which made Marion Davies' celebrated beach house at Santa Monica resemble nothing so much as a squatter's shack in the less residential section of the Jersey City marshes. Its resources were up to anything including typhoons, volcano eruptions, and life-size representations of the Battle of Austerlitz, and a staff of eight house carpenters was actually in residence throughout the Florida season repairing the tangible ravages of the most recent gala and making provision against the next.

Miami, at this time, was, of course, a community so bedizened as to make any other American Faubourg seem approximately as solvent as a Confederate shinplaster. Its villas were gaudier, its motor-cars more gleaming, its millionaires more millionairish, its gamblers more John L. Gates-ish, and its gem robberies more true to the E. Phillips Oppenheim originals than could be found anywhere this side of Paramount Pictures studios. Barton was the ranking dreamer-upper of pageants and charades for the most lavishly upholstered dudes, duchesses, and blue-sky refugees in this neo-Babylonish midst, and there were no accountants to scratch off items of four extra name bands from the bill or raise a vulgar eyebrow at the mere importation from Hawaii of a full carload of pineapples as atmosphere for an evening in Waikiki, as though the Miami moon and wonderful Atlantic a hundred yards away weren't props enough. Everything was the best. It was imported.

Life at the Bagnio Barton undulated pleasantly to ground swells of Clicquot and Bollinger served in jeroboams, English cuvée; grilled South American quail and plovers' eggs were the native equivalent of hamburger and hotdogs at the simplest buffet luncheon; house footmen in royal livery drilled by the platoon in any of the several patios at all hours, and the merest cocktail levee at the Surf had its details been available to the editors of the *Daily Worker,* would have caused their blood pressure to mount to the giddy heights usually reserved only for May Day.

Barton himself, although the record indicates him to be in the vicinage of fifty, appears forty, acts thirty, and has the ingenuous enthusiasm for Pain's fireworks of twenty. His eyes gleam at the idea of fifty French waiters in blackface and otherwise disguised as Indian servants, wheeling in ice elephants of gigantic stature filled with fresh caviar at forty dollars a pound, and the merest hint will send him about planning a full-dress facsimile of the last stand of Napoleon, with all the guests charging full tilt off the porch at midnight to represent the destruction of Marshal Ney's cavalry in the sunken road at Waterloo.

Toward the end Palm Beach and its somewhat stuffier plushiness got the go-by in favor of Miami Beach from the Jim Farleys, Dwight Fiskes, Esmond O'Briens, George Washington Cavanaughs, and other glamour folk and swollen livers of the New York glitter scene. The Hugh Dillmans, Gladys Swarthouts, Lucius Boomers, and Nick Schenks found Barton just the thing to cheer them up during the pallid Januaries in Manhattan, and around the pools (there were several at the Surf), footmen flooded the professional names of Broadway and Bel Air with ardent waters, and it was jestingly remarked that Alfred's mink and monocle guests wore out a full set of gold service plates every three years.

The Saturday night galas were the Surf's first claim to immortality, and it was in them that Barton's genius for running up super-charades found its fullest expression. From his own sketches the lounge and pools of the premises were transformed on successive weeks of the Florida season into the Taj Mahal, a trailer camp, the preview of the New York World's Fair, the last days of Pompeii, the French court at Versailles. As a matter of fact, upon the occasion of the Taj Mahal party, it was found expedient to erect three huge facsimiles of the temple itself at the extremities of the three pools, so that guests might invite each other to come and fall into the bath most conveniently adjacent to *their* table, after sampling the merits of the other two.

For a trailer-camp party, Barton rounded up scores and scores of ancient and battered jaloppies from near-by Florida boneyards, all of them in working order, and the guests drove themselves merrily around the lobbies and galleries of the club in disintegrating T Model heaps, oversetting tables and dowagers and colliding amidst fountains and hysterical explosions of shattered glass, spare parts, and debutantes. There was a brisk trade in arnica and bandages next day, and the local medical profession heartily endorsed this novel departure from the conventional costume party, which seldom resulted in any such gratifying quantities of head wounds and mayhem.

Only occasionally has Barton been thwarted in the magnitude or spaciousness of his aims. One of these was at the time of the Taj Mahal party, when it was revealed, and very cross it made him, too, that no door in the club was large enough to admit a small packtrain of elephants he had arranged for the occasion. Next time he has a club built there'll be no such shortsighted architect employed, you may be sure.

For a dinner given a few years ago by a spark-plug satrap from Detroit, Barton had imported an airplane load of lobsters from Gloucester, not for eating purposes—heaven forbid anything as utilitarian and unimaginative as that—but as decorations for a mousse of English sole which was an integral part of the menu. At the Surf, too, he displayed a fine Italian hand in inventing costly little elegances and never missed an opportunity to serve water ices, one to a guest, in individual pineapples, or to have tables for three hundred built of ice so frozen as not to drip and the gelid depths of each block decorated with rare orchids frozen in. It was a tenet of the Miami creed that if any one were ever so coarse as to command a pork chop at the Surf, a whole roast pig would be served up and all but the single chop at once tossed into the Gulf Stream.

Barton began his career as a latter-day Petronius to Woodrow Wilson's tour of France at the conclusion

Only occasionally has Barton been thwarted

of one of the various world wars some years ago. His actual rank was that of aide-de-camp to General W. W. Harts in Paris, and the road company of American officialdom was generally admitted to be an admirably routed series of stands, while the President achieved a reputation for protocol and promptness largely through the coaching and adroit elbow-jogging of the elegant Alfred. Colonel Edward House was adviser on affairs of state, and Alfred was supervisor of punctilio.

The township of Surfside at Miami Beach, in which the Surf Club was and still is located as its bright particular jewel, has only about three hundred voters, and a very closed corporation they used to be, too. There were no provisions for pedestrians in Surfside, since every one there was expected to own his own motor, and armed guards stopped all pedestrians on principle and demanded their identification. All domestics, both private and in clubs, were finger-printed and checked with Federal authorities, and, although Miami proper seethed with imported gunmen and what the Hearst papers were pleased to call "international jewel thieves," there never was a robbery of note at the Surf.

Barton caused the erection of a sort of Richardson Wright–*Town and Country* jail at Surfside. The cells had Beautyrest mattresses on every bunk, Venetian blinds, hot and cold running water, crested stationery, and an electric kitchenette for the preparation of midnight snacks. This elegant pokey was, however, no Big Rock Candy Mountain of the hobo's dream, since guests practically had to dress for dinner to achieve admission, and the Surfside cops, who were tough and ornery, tossed the small fry over to the ragpicker squad in

Miami, where things were very rough sledding indeed and pheasant hardly ever on the menu.

Once it fell to Barton's lot to arrange in New York's Waldorf-Astoria an out-of-the-Florida-season dinner for an organization known as the Committee of one hundred, a posse of Miami nobs, very few of whom ever saw Florida except between December and March. The component parts of this minor tumult included an entire trainload of Florida palm trees, George Ade, a railroad tank car filled with live pampano and stone crabs, William K. Vanderbilt, an entire floor at the Waldorf, and two hundred barrels of genuine Biscayne Bay sand and an orange grove. The tank car of seafood, along with the thirty-foot palms, presented something of a problem for executives of the Seaboard Air Line, but, with Harvey Firestone, Gar Wood, Frank Gannett, Fred F. Fisher, Sebastian Kresge, Charles F. Kettering, and Dr. John Oliver La Gorce footing the bill this was only a minor consideration, and the thicket of palm trees was hoisted up the Park Avenue façade of the Waldorf and snaked in a window in jig time. It was later removed in smaller and handier sections.

It is not beyond the dreams of imagination that Barton's genius may, one of these days, be again in demand at the Surf or elsewhere and his private entertainments revive the glories of Mardi Gras in New Orleans or the Battle of Trafalgar. He was recently encountered in New York's Plaza Hotel muttering about a post-war pageant depicting the history of civilization from earliest recorded times down to the inaugural of Chester A. Arthur, with a score by Virgil Thomson. He has always had a secret hanker for portraying the Burning of Rome and the signing of the Concordat of Worms, and he feels both these events can be included in the larger tapestry. Also, he could fill swimming pools with crocodiles to represent Nero's gardens. One of these days he's going to reproduce the Creation right out of Genesis, only six times as brilliant in its concept as the original, and when Alfred says *"Fiat Lux,"* the populace will be quick to reach for its sun glasses. The first evolution of the universe will be as a third Shubert road company in comparison with his version of it.

Another of the mayors of the palace who must bulk large in any record of screwball luxe of recent years was George Lamaze, a skillet and stewpot fellow of fantastic proportions, since gone to his reward and doubtless toying with oysters Rockefeller and foie gras in aspic in some celestial patio, small, chic, and very, very expensive.

Like Byfield and Barton, Lamaze combined eating and drinking with a first-rate sense of showmanship and was aware that the most commonplace dish or drink, if conveyed to its ultimate consumer by powdered flunkies and with strains of the Flonzaley Quartette playing "Pomp and Circumstance," was possessed of a double enchantment and could be retailed for at least four times the price.

As a luxury merchant Lamaze was more than a gustatory visionary, an international impresario of frogs' legs Provençales and mignonettes de bœuf Bordelaise, a dreamer-up of routs for the princes of the world. He was the first man to evolve the combination of cold boiled pompano with mustard sauce; he improved the classic French formula for chestnut soup, and Joseph

Hergesheimer speaks reverently of his Palm Beach restaurant (where bread and butter were a dollar a plate) as the "shrine and birthplace of sauce Lamaze and stone crabs." He was a ribald, mellow, and gorgeous fellow, who would give you his shirt or a Mickey Finn with equal readiness, depending on his esteem for you, but if any one spoke of him as a "genial host," he retired to the men's room and was ill for hours.

Lamaze's mother was the most celebrated cook of her generation in Rheims, and when George landed at Castle Garden he carried with him something of her stewpot genius. He was graduated from Brown and in 1907 got his first job as wine boy at Café Martin, which he always recalled as the finest restaurant in the world at that time. Although he subsequently worked in varying capacities at the Holland House, Rectors, the Folies-Bergère, and a number of establishments of his own contriving, Café Martin always had a lien on his deepest affection.

Concessions to mediocrity or popular taste could not be discovered in the Lamaze dossier. Of the Folies-Bergère, which was located where the Fulton Theater now stands and was operated by Henry B. Harris, who lost his life on the *Titanic,* he said: "The spot was twenty years ahead of its time. If we had filled the theater restaurant twice a night we couldn't have paid the salaries. We opened in June, 1911, and closed before snowfly, but you will see what a successful bankruptcy we were when I tell you that our cast included Laura Guerite, Ada Lewis, Ina Claire, Justine Johnson, Mae West (at thirty-five dollars a week), Laddie Cliff, Taylor Holmes, Arthur Lipson, Olga Petrova, Ethel Levy, Felix Adler,

Will Rogers, Otis Harlan, Nat Wills, La Belle Titcomb, Bernard Granville, Harry Pilcer (dancing with Minerva Coverdale), Grace LaRue, Carter de Haven, of *The Girl in the Taxi* fame, Martha L'Enclude, and the ballet from the Milan Opéra."

After the Folies-Bergère, he opened Castles by the Sea at Long Beach, N. Y., for the Vernon Castles, with Pierre, Louis Cantone, and Italo, a very well-known maître d'hôtel in those days. He was working at the Plaza when Mrs. John W. Gates offered five hundred dollars for the first member of the staff to enlist in the World War forces, and George was so quick to catch the prize that Mrs. E. H. Gary, of United States Steel fame, added a similar amount, so that he was one of the few who went to war with a thousand dollar bonus in advance.

After the war, Mr. Lamaze began to realize his gaudiest ambitions in the way of de luxe restaurant proprietorship. He took over El Carmelo in Havana for the winter season of 1919-20 and waltzed up a menu where wine was a flat twenty-five dollars and Arroz con Pollio five dollars a portion, but even these spendthrift prices were transcended when he returned to an allegedly dry New York and operated the Palais Royale, the Plantation, and the Little Club in the brave days of Charlie Journal and a slender Paul Whiteman. He knew he had arrived when he was able to charge and, what's more, get seven dollars a pint for White Rock and thirty-five dollars up for a bottle of Hackensack Meadows champagne.

His greatest triumph of the twenties was, of course, the celebrated Patio Lamaze, where he went into business with Wilson Mizner in the Via Mizner at Palm Beach. The writer still recalls the glories of its menu in the great days of the social battle between Mrs. Edward T. Stotesbury and Mrs. Manville, when one million dollars cash passed across the tables every night at Jack Bradley's, when the Poinciana Hotel's tracks held thirty-five private Pullmans at a time and were always full, and when a modest dinner for two, without wine, could not be had at any Palm Beach restaurant for less than one hundred dollars. George was in his element with the dollar bread and butter and ten dollar asparagus and Huttons, Clarence Barron, Otto Kahn, and titled English moochers waiting for tables, even though Colonel Bradley did him one better by imposing a table couvert of twenty-five dollars which invariably appeared on the check as "charge for flowers." Later he ran the Clover Club in Hollywood, Arrowhead Inn at Saratoga, and the Beach and Tennis, down the line from Alfred Barton's princely Surf Club at Miami Beach, but the Patio Lamaze was always his greatest love, along with Café Martin, one of which he owned and in the other of which he was a bus.

Lamaze's last assignment, and one admittedly comparable to any of the more difficult tasks of Hercules, was to put the city of Philadelphia on the night-life map. It brought him to his grave, but it can not be said he failed, since, during his régime at least, the Warwick Hotel became at once a gustatory Mecca and a temple of such mirth and chivalry as the Main Line could boast or Lamaze himself import. He evolved a number of "Stork Club" and "Monte Carlo" and "El Morocco" evenings, and New Yorker name bands and other transplanted celebrities made night hideous and wonderful in the neighborhood of Rittenhouse Square.

On such occasions everything on the menu was more than vaguely reminiscent of the master himself: eggs Lamaze, oysters Lamaze, soufflé Lamaze, sauce Lamaze, asparagus Lamaze, and crêpes Lamaze, and sooner or later George was accustomed to make an entry in person, surrounded by flaming brochettes of chicken liver or popping out of an enormous lamb pot pie (Lamaze). Later at night these levees were accustomed to expand in a quite un-Philadelphia-like manner over the surrounding community, ending at the Embassy Club, of perfumed memory, or Benny the Bum's. Sunday was invariably spent counting and nursing sprains, contusions, and lacerations received at the hands of treacherous stairways, petulant pavements, and refractory bedposts, and ascertaining the probable whereabout of misplaced husbands, mink coats, and automobiles. For once in its history Philadelphia had its day—and night.

20

A DAY WITH
MISS CARROLL

So you want to know about a day in the life of a film actress on the town in the spacious times when the words gasoline, T-bone steak, and champagne were not qualified in the Oxford Dictionary as "obsolete"? Well, children, your grandfather used to get around a bit then, dropping into the Union League for a quick one with Philip Hone before going to the horse show at the old Madison Square Garden with Jenny Lind, Mayor A. Oakey Hall, and Mamie Fish—or is he getting his period designs mixed? Anyway, you must believe everything happened just as he tells you, no matter how improbable it seems, because there were giants in those days.

Well, a day in Manhattan, where Miss Madeleine Carroll paused briefly before treating herself to a New Year's Eve in Paris after finishing a film called *Café Society* for Paramount, began about the time the Twentieth Century Limited was changing engines at Harmon, say, *circa* eight in the morning. Miss Carroll was still snoozing comfortably, and one hopes prettily, in her suite aboard the Pullman Schuylkill Valley, albeit her tiring maids were up drawing tea and laying out I. Magnin street suits for her to choose from; but in Manhattan a number of folk were, contrary to every use and custom, up and doing. Mr. Bob Gilham, of Paramount, was phoning in a last-moment frenzy to find out if Miss Carroll was arriving on the Central or maybe the Pennsy. Mr. Douglas Gilbert, of the *World-Telegram,* was looking at himself in the shaving mirror and re-marked quietly: "Gilbert, you give me a pain in the neck!" Paramount's Mr. Al Wilkie was changing from a dinner-jacket to street clothes so as not to make his day look like a papal reception. The reporter was being awakened in his hack by a Vestris cab driver from the corner of Fortieth and Seventh, who said, "Come, come, Mr. Beebe, this is no way to welcome La Belle Made-leine!" Quite a number of photographers in various locales were putting packs of Pancro-Press 4x5's in their pockets and cursing nine-o'clock assignments. The Cen-tury had just been given green at Spuyten Duyvil when all these scrambled personalities converged on the plat-form of Track 26 at Grand Central, and the day was on.

Miss Carroll, pretty as a picture (she is a picture, you dope), started her day with a brisk twenty-minute rou-tine of peering coyly from Pullman windows, posing, waving tan capeskin mitts from vestibules, and other-wise comporting herself as is expected amid a heat-lightning barrage of photographers' flares. Shortly there-after she was welcomed as no royalty is ever received at the doorway of the Ritz by Mr. Albert Keller, the man-aging director himself, in a braided frock coat with rosettes at every buttonhole. The scene called for four policemen, fifteen photographers, four or five reporters, half a dozen Paramount executives, six house footmen tottering under the loads of luggage, a mob of autograph solicitors—oh, and Miss Madeleine Carroll. The whole shebang produced by Al Wilkie, of Paramount, and directed by Bob Gilham.

By ten o'clock, and against all the laws of probability, Miss Carroll had achieved her suite in the Ritz and contrived to cut down her retinue to a mere three Paramount satraps and two interviews, including Mr. Douglas Gilbert, who didn't feel so badly now about his lost sleep. Miss Carroll wanted to take a bath, but the afternoon papers couldn't wait, so everybody had breakfast, mostly croissants and coffee, and at eleven o'clock she really hoped to be able to get into her tub, when a fresh delegation of reporters arrived. At a quarter of twelve she had her hand practically on the doorknob when the floodgates of the New York Telephone Company were unloosed, and a deluge of distance calls poured in from Paris, London, Hollywood, Chicago, and darkest Pelham Manor.

Promptly at one o'clock there was announced Miss Eileen Creelman, of the *Sun*, for an interview and a brace of lamb chops, and the bath was dismissed as a mere humorous improbability. After Miss Creelman came Tom Waller, of Paramount, with an A. P. feature writer and six photographers from national syndicates, and the two carloads of them were whirled to Macy's, where Miss Carroll was to be photographed doing her Christmas shopping. The mob scene that ensued was one of the day's more epic convulsions. The people cheered, the people screamed, the people demanded autographs, photographs, and attention. House detectives ran up blood pressures of positively Union League proportions, and a showcase filled with costume jewelry disintegrated with a fascinating crash under mob pressure. In the end the party made a getaway and ran over to a shop run by the institute for the blind, where shopping was less like the Astor Place riots.

By half-past three Miss Carroll was back at the Ritz, a trifle disheveled and plaintively suggesting that perhaps she would be permitted to take a bath. This witticism was greeted by a chorus of horse laughs, however, and there arrived Miss Aileen Brenon, of Paramount, who brought up Katherine Albert, of *Photoplay*, for an interview, after which, as a special treat, Miss Carroll was photographed in color by Ruzzie Green for *McCall's*, a long and trying performance only equaled as a fatigue irritant by the business of fitting clothes.

At 6:15 happy splashing announced that Miss Carroll had at last achieved her bath, and afterward she was allowed fifteen whole minutes in which to lie down before the reporter arrived to convey her to a performance of *Leave It to Me*.

"Now, remember," Mr. Wilkie had said sternly. "Dinner at '21' at 7; the Imperial at 8:45; Chez Firehouse for John Krimsky's party at 11:30; Morocco at midnight; the Stork at 12:45, 1:30 at Versailles, 2 o'clock at the Onyx, and sharp at 2:30 for the last show at Jack White's. After that you can have the evening to yourselves, but there will be photographers spotted, and I want no nonsense or getting off schedule."

Whether it is done with mirrors or how, nobody knows, but after a day of excitements and distractions which would have floored a long-shoreman, Miss Carroll seemed ready to take on the world, and said as much. At Jack and Charlie's she greeted with courtesy and enthusiasm a dozen or so acquaintances, three or four of whom she even knew by name, and sat down to a dinner of oysters Rockefeller with an Amoroso sherry, gray-legged Scotch grouse and a Grand Montrachet, boldly asserting that she preferred a white Burgundy to a red, and proving it by finishing the bottle to the last drop; and ending with an artichoke and butter and a bottle of Perrier-Jouet 1919, which Bob Kriendler had unbelievably dug up from the deepest bins in the house.

Miss Carroll's dinner was, to be sure, punctuated by two transatlantic telephone calls which she took at the table, asserting that no phone call was worth interrupting dinner for anyway, and proving herself a conversationalist and gourmet of perceptiveness and authentic charm.

Her arrival at the Imperial Theatre was the signal for a skirmish with the people second only to the afternoon's scuffle at Macy's, and by actual count she signed thirty-five autograph books before being permitted to get into the house. The intermission was almost as bad when she attempted a quick safari to the Piccadilly Bar, where, while the author lapped up two nervous cognacs, she absorbed an unruffled pot of coffee before venturing out to engage the signature fiends once more.

True to schedule, Miss Carroll arrived promptly at 11:30 at the party given by the brothers Krimsky, John and Jerrold, in the grand manner for an unknown debutante who had been secured for the occasion from the Powers model catalogue. Every arrival was an-

nounced from the door by Harry Meehan, the Irish
Thrush, as "Mr. and Mrs. J. Dinsmore Tew," an introduction which provided the only point in a slightly
demented evening at which Miss Carroll looked just a
bit alarmed. The Krimsky debutante party proved an
elaborate parody of the real thing, with a receiving line
fifteen deep and a profusion of opera-length gloves,
orchid corsages, powdered footmen, and white ties.

At once beset by every unattached man on the premises, she danced with Alfred de Liagre, waltzed madly
with Jules Glaenzer and announced that Peter Arno
was the wickedest-looking man in New York. She posed
for innumerable photographs, chatted professionally
with Brock and Margaret Pemberton, applauded handsomely for John Hoysradt's impersonations, drank a
substantial quantity of champagne with the reporter
and declared she was on vacation, no longer in training,
and was going to have herself a good time. The stag line
allowed her approximately thirty seconds with each
dance partner. Jerrold Krimsky squired her gallantly
around to practically every table in the room. She stood
among the stags at the bar for an appreciable time with
Jaro Fabry and danced all over again with Mr. de Liagre,
who enjoyed more of her company than any one else
present.

It was just three o'clock when she first looked at her
watch and declared hastily that, goshamighty, she ought
to be in bed, because the first interviewer was due at
nine in the morning. Alas for El Morocco, alas for the
Stork. Bed claimed her, as it probably had long since
the cameramen awaiting her advent at the Onyx and
Jack White's. Just a sample day in the life of a film

Everybody was Mr. and Mrs. J. Dinsmore Tew

celebrity, the reporter remarked to himself as he tottered home, thankful for the tranquillity of the existence of a Broadway paragrapher.*

* The urgencies of the war effectively removed Miss Carroll from the midst of tinsel fakements to which she had professionally accustomed herself. After her nineteen-year-old sister was killed in a London air raid, she found her time increasingly devoted to good works, the most notable of which were her activities as Chairman of the National Entertainment Committee of the United Seaman's Services. She married Sterling Hayden, a film actor, who changed his name to John Hamilton in order to achieve anonymity and a career in the United States Marine Corps, and is credited with numerous unidentifiable wartime charities and generosities. One of these, which has been authenticated for the record, is the support in her home near Paris of fifty-odd war orphans. Her sympathies lie most strongly, however, with the less exploited activities of merchant seamen.

21

ONE-GULCH JACK

It isn't Julesburg, Colorado, which once was proud to advertise itself as "the wickedest city in America," or Laramie or Cheyenne or Rawlins with their legends of the U. P. trail in the spacious days of Jack Casement and the railroad builders, or Denver or Leadville or Central City, fragrant with bonanza souvenirs, or even the cow towns of Texas with their sagas of border chivalry and unforgotten six-gun doings, that is the most frontier-conscious vicinage of the countryside. The Saturday night slugging and shooting may be powerful tough at Roger's Stables in Palm Springs; Amon Carter may ceaselessly promote Fort Worth as the archetype of he-man towns; the cowboy atmosphere be never so thick as among the dude ranches and rodeos of Colorado and Wyoming, but, speaking in hyperbole, the shotgun messengers ride hardest toward Boot Hill in West Fifty-second Street, the Borough of Manhattan, New York City.

For nowhere else in North America is the sagebrush legend and an atmosphere of boots and saddles so assiduously cultivated as among the cowboys of Gotham and adjacent eastern communities, and the frontier of the Old West pales by comparison with the florid attire, the red-blooded personalities, and the swift action of the hands who gather at sundown at Jack and Charlie's in a midst of wagon wheels, branding irons, and tall tales of cattle rustling. Not even the old scout doings at Mac's Hitch Rack Saloon adjacent to the Fleischaker Pool outside San Francisco can compare, on a brisk week-end, with the rompin' and stompin' at "21."

The emergence on the Fifty-second Street horizon of Two Gun (sometimes after midnight known as One Gulch) Jack Kriendler as the dressiest of American cowboys, not even excepting luminaries in fur trousers such as Paul Whiteman and Gene Autrey, has covered a period of years and has engaged the attention of students of social institutions to a considerable degree. Kriendler in early-prohibition times was no more distinguished around town than any other hard-working restaurateur in a notably successful partnership, but he was always a rogue at heart and was possessed of a hanker for spacious and gaudy gestures, and of recent years, with every sort of success and security achieved, he began to blossom out as a very orchidaceous fellow indeed. It manifested itself first in the country club up Mount Kisco way which wasn't any great success as a financial venture and folded after two seasons, but it gave Jack an opportunity to wear some of the fanciest clothes on record, and he counted it money well lost. To-day he runs to such checks, stripes, plaids, and over-plaids, such Charvet cravats and snuff-colored waistcoats as haven't been seen since the old Broadway days of George Kessler and Berry Wall. He loves to give splendid dinner parties where, both by virtue of being host and by a real feeling for comedy, he can sing solos and make speeches like crazy. He has instituted a series of special annual feasts like his "Founders' Dinner" and "Lonely Hearts' Party" that are town institutions, and one of his favorite gestures is the hiring of large orchestras to accompany him around town in the small hours and complement his singing of sentimental ballads. Christmas night he recruited twenty-five Salvation Army musicians playing nothing but silver cornets and serenaded John Perona at El Morocco until Perona donated a very substantial sum to the Army cause.

But Jack's greatest weakness is the glamorous West. He went to Palm Springs a few winters ago, and ever since then existence at "21" has been a combination of restaurant de luxe and life on the range. He has more cowboy accessories than Abercrombie and Fitch ever dreamed of and wouldn't be surprised if his western wardrobe, including saddles and such, had set him back fifty thousand dollars to date.

Some years ago, at the opening of the Golden Gate Exposition as the San Francisco World's Fair was known, Jack was on hand for the fiesta which occupied three days of municipal howling and roaring before the opening of the fair itself. San Francisco was celebrated for its parades, and Jack was celebrated for never missing one, and he was made a marshal by the city fathers, who were grateful for his good offices and colorful person, not to mention his maintenance of a free-for-every-one champagne bar at the Mark Hopkins

Hotel and the support of his comings and goings with brass bands in his own employ.

For the occasion Jack had run up a fabulous cowboy saddle, the handiwork of a notable saddler, Porter of Tucson, which set him back a cool five thousand dollars. As a bemused spectator in Powell Street remarked, no-

He advocates the rugged way of life

body had ever seen a silver saddle with so many leather trimmings. But schism reared its head when it became bruited in the public prints that Mrs. Elizabeth Altemus Whitney, something of a cowgirl in her own right and not averse to publicity, planned to ride in the great parade sporting a saddle with even fewer leather trimmings, which had cost her twenty thousand dollars! Livid with chagrin, Jack brooded among the wine flagons in his suite on the top of Nob Hill. Friends could not comfort him or even the photographers restore his accustomed equanimity. Achilles was sulking in his ten-room-and-six-baths tent. At long last he had it! Mrs. Whitney could never rank Kriendler, and calling for his mount he was off to the parade in Market Street.

It was a momentous triumph, for Jack rode in four different spots in the parade, and didn't that, at five thousand dollars per saddle appearance, just tie him with Mrs. Whitney, who appeared only once with twenty thousand dollar trappings?

Rodeo Ben of the wild ranges of Columbia Avenue, Philadelphia, makes most of the western and riding clothes for professionals of the stage, films, dude ranches, and rodeos, just as Heiser, of Kansas City, makes the most spectacular belts, holsters, saddles, and leather equipment, and it is Ben's opinion that Mr. Kriendler is the best-dressed amateur cowboy in the land. The cynical might suggest that Mr. Kriendler achieves this nomination the way some title-holders come by the name "best-dressed woman"—through virtue of the greatest expenditure on wardrobe.

But any one who has ever seen Two Gun Jack in Palm Springs or anywhere else west of the Mississippi has to admit he cuts a mighty fine figger of a frontiersman. Even while servicing the upholstered patrons at "21" Jack is likely to sport under his faultless morning clothes a heavily bossed cowboy belt with a gold buckle, and high-heeled Mexican boots have occasionally been seen peeping from under his evening trousers.

Among others named by Rodeo Ben is Albert Hernig, of Bustleton, Pa., a retired and wealthy Keystone Stater, who spends from ten to twenty-five dollars on his shirts and up to fifty dollars for his closely fitted Mexican riding trousers. Also in the running is Tom Endicott, who owns and operates the Dude Ranch Night Club at Atlantic City. New Yorkers have, of course, long been familiar with Paul Whiteman's Western wardrobe, which he enjoys showing off on horseback in Central Park, while the dandiest frontier dresser in all the Southwest is the legendary Amon G. Carter, of Fort Worth, who eschews cowboy clothes in favor of oldtime cattlemen's formal outfits—dovegray or black-and-white-checked morning coats, white Stetsons, and pearl-handled guns on either hip.

Rodeo Ben says that the notion that a "dude" cowboy outfits himself without reference to realism or good taste is entirely fallacious. "The Easterner's knowledge and experience with clothing and workmanship," he says, "give him a critical eye in purchasing fine Western clothes to suit his whim and fancy. That the colors involved are sometimes flashier than would be in accordance with more moderate taste is merely a professional requirement." About the most costly single item of Western dress Rodeo Ben makes up is the conventional short riding jacket, something like a mess jacket, matching the riding trousers, which comes as high as one hundred and fifty dollars. Mr. Kriendler's Western wardrobe is replete with sixty dollar shirts, and there are whole closets devoted solely to the storage of Stetson Seven X Beavers, the last word in fashionable plainsman's attire, which retail at around one hundred and twenty-five dollars apiece.

Other notables in the ranks of Manhattan's riders of the purple sage, when occasion, publicity, or their whim requires it, include Peter Arno, John Reid Topping, younger brother of Bob Topping and known locally as the Cisco Kid, Ham Fisher, James Montgomery Flagg, Messmore Kendall, and George Fitts, but none of them are quite in a class with One-Gulch Jack.

In the middle of dinner hour at "21," when most of his clientele, attired in white tie and tails, are en route to the opera, Kriendler can be discovered in the lobby practising drawing a frontier-model Colt and rolling cigarettes from a Bull Durham sack with the other hand. He gives dinners of venison and buffalo meat and antelope steaks, and his gifts to friends are invariably of western or Palm Springs origin. Make no mistake, he will pass into the New York legend along with such picaresque figures as Wouter Van Twiller, A Oakey Hall, and such latter-day individualists as Manny Chappelle, Center Hitchcock, Diamond Jim Brady, and Freddy Gebhard.

22

ONE-MAN U.S.O.

THE day after Pearl Harbor, my room-mate, Chuck Clegg, with whom I shared an apartment in Fifty-eighth Street and who was a departmental executive at Arnold Constable's, enlisted in the Naval Reserve, and there began an interlude, not yet drawing to any definite conclusion, which I think of as my war with the United States Navy.

Chuck felt very strongly about the war and wanted to be in on it at once. The pattern of his personal honor was uncomplicated by any of the Social Register overtones and considerations which committed the patriotic efforts of so many of our acquaintances to stylish skirmishes for commissions, and which made life a weariness for their congressmen and rich fathers-in-law. The Navy was offering ratings and assorted inducements to all sorts of technicians, who were in great requisition, and the room-mate was a radio ham of impressive proportions, having been making active passes at the wireless since the days of crystal detectors. He was also bored with signing charge-credit slips for yap-yap mammas from the Bronx and otherwise filling his department-store obligations and, urgently purposeful as he was about the armed services, he was possessed of a happy naïveté which enabled him to extract pleasure or amusement from almost anything. I have never known misfortune, inconvenience, or even the idiot conduct in high places encountered by every military person to make the least dent in his even temper and kindness of disposition. And it was obvious that the Navy was infinitely preferable to the sordid life of the foot soldiery.

The Navy accepted him with, I gathered, glad acclaim, a circumstance attested by subsequent promotions and favors. But I had no way of knowing that when Chuck became a radio technician I was by way of becoming a one-man U.S.O.

Flushed and triumphant he returned home that evening.

"I'm in," he announced with the air of one who has been made a Morgan partner and twisting the foil from a bottle of wine which he had retrieved from the icebox. "I'm just to sit around near a telephone and they're to call me in a day or two!"

I was impressed and touched and felt there was no time to be lost. He might be on the high seas tomorrow night. "Quick," I said, "change your clothes and we'll go out on the town. It's going to be the goddamnedest farewell party you ever heard of!"

That was how little either of us knew about war in general and the Navy in particular.

The next day was Tuesday the ninth and, nursing a brace of museum-piece hangovers, we were in pyjamas in the drawing-room drinking a double bottle of Perrier Jouet and moaning softly when the phone rang.

"That's probably for me," said the room-mate. "God knows, nothing that can happen in battle will be any worse than this, but I hate to leave home looking like something prefabricated for sea burial."

It was not, however, the President calling him to the colors, but Howard Barnes announcing that New York was going to be bombed by air raiders in two hours—it had just come in over the news services at the shop—and would we be lunching at the Colony or Jack and Charlie's when the city was blown to smithereens? We settled for "21," and so, seemingly, did every one else in New York. Marion Tiffany Saportas, Mrs. Orson Munn, Prince Serge Obolensky, the Gilbert Millers, and Beth Leary when we arrived were offering Philip the ransom of princes for our regular table from which, presumably, to take off for a better and more fashionable world. We were barely seated with fifteen minutes to spare before the de luxe detonations were scheduled to start when a cloud of news photographers from the *Journal-American,* the *Daily News* and Acme descended on the scene and it was apparent that the invasion was going to be a social success.

"You'll never enlist in another war like this," remarked Cole Porter from an adjacent position of vantage, and Chuck said he was sure he wouldn't and ordered a hand set run to the table in case the Secretary of the Navy should call him in the hour of crisis. John Byram, from Paramount Pictures, the Grand Duchess Marie, Louis Sobol, and Ted Husing arrived just under the wire, positively panting for their professional reputations. It was a very pleasant and exciting lunch, pregnant with expectancy and eventual anticlimax, but it gave the room-mate a satisfactory sense of being already in combat, and every one bought him dozens of farewell drinks, so that he was returned home late that afternoon, practically on a shutter.

From then on we lived with telephones at hand and all the phone operators in town apprised of our momentary whereabouts, and were sure that every call was from the Navy in urgent need of its newest radio technician, second class. Trailing telephone wires and a vague aura of well-being, we kept available to 90 Church Street for several weeks. The farewell salvos thundered in the best bars, and the number of free drinks he absorbed from grateful fellow countrymen and even, when he was feeling gracious, British majors and Colonial colonels, numbered in the thousands. Barmen at the Coq Rouge and the Stork got a sort of haven't-you-gone-away-yet look in their eyes as we approached and, since nothing but champagne was considered suitable as an off-to-the-wars drink, our bills at Sherry's, Bellows, and other wine merchants were becoming the subject of credit-rating investigations. Rumors spread around the better night clubs that it was all a hoax to rate free drinks from the management or at the expense of bemused patriots, and that Chuck hadn't really joined the Navy at all.

Things were becoming drastic when, after a full month and just about the time public enthusiasm for his sacrifice was wearing thin, word actually came that the roomy was to report for duty the next morning. This was the real thing. This was it. We might not see each other again for years, and not a deadfall in Fifty-second Street but felt the impact of his going. At six in the morning, barrelled to the hat, we parted. Happy landings, kid. Let me know where you are as soon as you can. Wear your Christopher medal. So long, baby, keep your nose clean.

Then silence. Or comparatively since I sniffed while shaving because I liked my roomy and felt like hell to see him going away.

The silence of military secrecy lasted until five-thirty that evening, when the door of the apartment was splintered on its hinges and Chuck, in an outsize sailor's suit and beaming from ear to ear, made an entry. He was in the Navy, but the Navy had no place to put him and he was home, for the moment anyway.

Reason totters at the recollection of the subsequent period when the United States Naval Reserve took over Fifty-eighth Street in its entirety and the hotel staff gradually and painfully acquired a seagoing vocabulary. The floor, a handy place to fall until then, became the deck. The stairways became ladders. The bath-room, previously known as the can or Harvard Room, became the head. To go downstairs was below decks, and meals were changed to chow. Our dresser had to learn to tie a proper square knot for an issue scarf and floor waiters were reported to announce, in other people's apartments, that chow was served, madam.

The matter of uniforms alone was a major problem. Our dresser, perfectly accustomed to pouring the room-mate into morning or evening clothes, sports attire, or whatever the occasion required, was totally baffled and thwarted by the Navy blouse and wide trousers which are required to be pressed inside out so that the creases are reversed from those intended by God and customary in civilian attire. This caused a great deal of confusion. So, eventually, did the tailor-made blues which, in fashionable enlisted circles, are cut to conform to the person of their possessor as a cupcake to its mold and require from three to five people to adjust to their wearer. Among Navy associates this is easily accomplished, every one taking turns helping insinuate his neighbor into his blouse, but at home it was a different proposition, and I often wrestled on the carpet, assisted by the floor waiter and two bellmen in an effort to get Chuck dressed for the evening. The sartorial effect, once accomplished, was highly satisfactory and caused anguish to the hearts of many a commissioned person attired in a blue bank clerk's suit, but there were nights when the roomy found it expedient to sleep in his uniform, knowing that he and I alone were no match for it and that small assistance could be expected at six in the morning when he had to return to his ship.

There is need for no more than the barest outline of the ensuing weeks, each evening characterized by one more anticlimactic farewell-forever party. They are imperishably recorded on a hundred waiter captains' reservations books, police blotters, and first-night lists. Furthermore there is hardly a person in the United States who has not lived through similar military crises. There was the night, immediately after his having been called for service, that I retired, leaving Chuck on the town, only to be awakened an hour or two later by anguished screams for help from a Shore Patrol station in Times Square. Since it was the military police and not the accustomed law, there was hardly anything that I could do about it, but eventually it got straightened. It seemed that Charles, proud in his newest uniform, had dropped into the Astor bar for a quickie whereupon one of the barkeeps took a look at him and shouted for the Shore Patrol. "This guy was in here in a silk hat last week and now he's in a uniform," he deposed. "Must be a spy!"

There was the matter of the parrot and coconuts. Being the most sudden sailor extant, the room-mate was inclined to nautical excess. One evening in the Copacabana, a night club of tropical pretentions, his fancy was taken with a live parrot which was part of the decorative scheme and which, of course, was immediately presented him by the press agent for the premises, Jack Diamond, who threw in a festoon of coconuts to boot. It was Chuck's fancy to take these ornaments back to his ship with him next day and it was with difficulty that I dissuaded him from having his ear pierced for an earring to set off the ensemble.

"All sailors have parrots, you dope!" he said crossly when I suggested that the ship's guard or his immediate officers might take exception to this bit of Joseph Conrad whimsy. Strangely enough, they didn't, and his appearance the next morning was a great success with all of his professional associates. It went to his head and led, eventually, to getting tatooed and singing chanties.

His fastidiousness of attire and super-nautical correctness led to another contretemps not without its humorous overtones when, after Easter Parade on Fifth Avenue in 1942, the late and gallant Lt. Commander McClelland Barclay, surveying a congress of fashionables in the Sherry Netherland café, awarded Charles the prize for best dressed man. The haberdasher who donated the prizes hadn't considered the possibility of their being taken by a man in service

The parrot led to tattooing

and my roomy came home in triumph with three expensive Ascot morning cravats.

Then, too, there were businesses of protocol in the saloons which required adjusting. A few of the town's

waiter captains, inexperienced in the economy of wartime society, cherished a temporary delusion that commissioned persons ranked enlisted personnel in the
matter of tables and reservations. It was a delusion enthu-
siastically endorsed by a number of pretentious Army
and Navy wives, but almost never by officers themselves,
and the maîtres d'hôtel were soon schooled in manners.
When Alfred Gwynne Vanderbilt, long an ornament
of the plushier puddles, turned up in a boatswain's
mate's uniform, he wasn't to be discarded, even momentarily, in favor of some provincial colonel who, until
the week before, had never encountered a French menu.
Sherman Billingsley was among the first to impress upon
his staff that old and favored customers whose names
and persons had for years lent smart atmosphere to his
establishment were to be recognized in a private's uniform just as punctiliously as though they were in a
tailcoat, and the Stork has always, as a result, enjoyed
the enthusiastic patronage of the solvent and more personable gentleman rankers of all branches of the
service.

Eventually, however, the Battle of Fifty-eighth Street-
sur-Mer drew to a close and the Navy required the
room-mate in Stillwater, Oklahoma, precisely located,
like the admiral in Dwight Fiske's song, fifteen hundred
miles from either ocean. Stillwater, a pretty town, but
approximately a million miles from nowhere, was no
bargain to get to for week-ends, and furthermore, Oklahoma is, legally speaking, a dry state. Also the wife of
the local social arbiter, who had to be cultivated, had
inflated notions of elegance. She had been reading the
New Yorker and *Harper's Bazaar* and dreaming up

strange drinks quite outside the knowledge of ordinary folk.

Wednesday evening the phone would ring and Charles would whimper over the wires that she had just heard about stingers and there was no white crême de menthe in Oklahoma at any price, and Thursday would find me in a sample of the Wright Brother's folly, headed vaguely for Tulsa with two suitcases of prefabricated stingers or sidecars or whatever droll arrangement the louey-commander's wife had read about last. Tulsa was not without its charm. There was, for instance, a night club that had formerly been a gasoline filling station and beer flowed out of all the compressed air hoses. There was, too, an aged and highly solvent religious fanatic who haunted the public places of the town and took a great fancy to Charles. He labored under the impression that the roomy was a sort of sea-going clergyman. To the old gentleman, the radioman's insignia on his arm represented God's thunderbolts, and he was forever seeking us out and buying free drinks in the nearest saloon, of which, Oklahoma being a legally arid commonwealth, there was a generous multiplicity.

From Stillwater, after a few weeks of intensified mathematics, bridge whist with the louey-commander's wife, and beer drinking with Gene Hoyt, the chief of police, Charles was ordered to San Francisco, and life took on more normal aspects. We knew flocks of folk in the vicinage of Post Street and even if we hadn't it would still have been the most hospitable town in the world. His apartment in the Palace was flanked on one hand by Sophie Tucker, who was then playing the Trocadero, and on the other by Frank Farrell of the *World-Tele-gram* who was a louey of Marines and headed for the Islands, and the great farewell parties, abetted by Mayor Rossi, Tim Fleuger, Margaret Chung, and other scamps of importance were resumed with an intensity only possible in the shadow of Telegraph Hill. I contrived, somehow, to get back and forth across the continent between week-ends, and while I was at home in Manhattan answering the mail, the roomy would be doing whatever was suitable for the Navy. Even in wartime and subject, as is all California, to military panic, San Francisco maintained its characteristics as the most glittering of all American towns. Charlie Norris's hospitality at the Bohemian Club was as untrammeled as ever. Lunch in the Palm Court of the Palace was still a cut-throat business of getting tables. The cable cars ran, Izzy Gomez remembered how to mix a Pisco punch, and people were still talking about The Fire. Folk came and went by train and plane, and the lobby of the Fairmont at dinner time was alive with Gladys Swarthout, Miss Barrymore, Alfred Barton, and whatever visiting pompiers were available.

I never arrived at the airport or the Oakland Terminal but to discover that the room-mate had, in my temporary absence, contrived to take over the social community more completely than before. Waiter captains at the St. Francis and the Prado were forever rolling out better ringside tables on his appearance. The bar staff at the Top of the Mark kept a bin of Mumms, in assorted sizes, iced against his possible arrival. Even taxi cabs materialized at his whistle, a phenomenon otherwise achieved only by Mr. Rossi and

Charlie Crocker. The war, as fought in Market Street, was a pretty agreeable interlude.

We became stewed and tatooed in the worst and best places, spent Sundays lunching at the Cliff House with Josephine Hull, who was playing in the coast company of *Arsenic and Old Lace,* and rode the windsprung ponies back of Mac's Hitch Rack later in the day.

From San Francisco, Chuck's orders commanded him to a particularly secretive Navy laboratory in Washington, and the very best timing obtained throughout. Christmas Day Edmond Reider, managing director of the Palace, and Mrs. Reider gave a dinner for the roomy, and New Year's Eve we arrived in Chicago just in time to miss all possible train connections for Washington, so that the year 1943 came to us in the Pump Room and a blaze of Byfield's best brandy. The next week-end Evie McLean was giving an enormous ball in honor of practically nothing at her new Friendship in R Street, and there was every indication that the war was a social success foolish, as the French say. I had by this time traveled 80,000 rail miles and only God knew how many air miles, keeping up with the wars and, like DeWolf Hopper, felt when I got back to Fifty-eighth Street that I could never get to sleep unless somebody stood at the foot of the bed shaking it and throwing handfuls of cinders in my face.

Artemus Ward remarked that Harvard University was pleasantly and conveniently situated in the bar room of Parker's in School Street. Today the Federal government of the United States enjoys being centrally located in Jack and Charlie's in Fifty-second Street, so Washington saw little of us during anything but the business week. Due to the housing shortage in the Federal City, Chuck engaged to live on a decommissioned yacht tied up in the Yacht Basin and, as he had taken over the captain's suite, with sleeping accommodations for more than a few, life along the Potomac was something less than quiet when he was in residence. Major Douglas Parmentier, Major Henry Thompson Rowell, later one of the military governors of Sicily, Congressman Will Rogers, and assorted dignitaries of the Federal government came and went at all hours. Gin was on tap in a water cooler and sparkling wine was iced by the simple expedient of dropping it out the porthole on a line where it achieved a suitable chill in the waters below. His salon may not have sported so many generals as Evie McLean's at Friendship, but there was a great deal of laughing and playing games and there was one night when a fiercely mustached captain of cavalry undertook to recite all of Swinburne, Byron, and Sir Walter Scott from memory. We went to bed in the middle of "The Lay of the Last Minstrel" and Sunday morning, when a general groaning and screaming for ice water announced that the assembled chivalry was awaking to a palsied Sabbath, he was still going with undiminished vigor amidst the gaudy rhymes of "Don Juan."

There was, too, the matter of the gangplank connecting this ark to the dimmed-out Washington waterfront. In normal repose, it sloped, as God intended gangplanks should, at a gentle angle from the pier to the deck and was negotiable under all reasonable circumstances if you knew just where to find it. Sometimes, however, if its various halyards and securements became fouled it would rise with the tide and, instead of being available to the explorative midnight foot, deal the returning householder a treacherous sock on the chin. And there was the occasion when, over a week-end and for some sufficient reason, the yacht was temporarily towed away from its accustomed berth entirely. Charles returned from the stews and bagnios of Manhattan of a dark winter morning and walked with fine confidence into the harbor. The Yacht Basin was the closest my sailor room-mate had been to the sea up till then.

At long last, however, even the most exhausting naval engagement must be broken off. There was a final pyrotechnic lunch in the Pump Room, a westward passage on the City of San Francisco, a farewell lunch with Madame le baron Reider at the Palace, an ultimate bottle of wine at the Top of the Mark, and the mists of the Golden Gate shrouded the roomy's going into the wastes of the Pacific. His most recent letter as this goes to the printers chronicles dining, *faut de mieux,* off boiled parrot with the natives on some anonymous Solomon and a plaintive inquiry as to whether, while all sailors were supposed to have parrots, they were also supposed to eat them.

This brief tally of frivolities is no impeachment of the seriousness of purpose with which my room-mate approached the business of war or of a technical competence which has been officially recognized in a lonely and imponderably dangerous branch of service. It is merely a footnote to the business of the civilian manpower necessary and requisite for the proper support of individuals in the armed forces. The home front depends not only, such a survey would seem to reveal, upon the functions of chemists, turret-lathe workers, and welders, but also upon carriage starters and house footmen, barmen, maîtres d'hôtel and wine stewards. They, too, are elements of military morale.

23

ETYMOLOGICAL NOTE

T HIS is a blow-by-blow account of a stirring intellectual encounter between Valentina Schlee, and J. J. O'Donohue IV, the Park Avenue gallant, at the bar of the Metropolitan Opera House one evening during the ballet. It may serve as a study in contemporary English usage or double talk for future students of the language.

Joe and Valentina enter from opposite sides of the bar. They see each other. They rush stage center. They embrace.

Joe: Darling, darling!

Val: Sweet, sweet!

Joe: Drink? Drink?

Val: Sure, sure!

Joe: Haig-Haig?

Val: Haig-Haig.

Joe: Soda, soda?

Val: Splash, splash!

Joe: Hot night, darling!

Val: Putrid night, sweet!

Joe: What cooks?

Val: Nothing ghastly!

Joe: Oyster Bay?

Val: Oyster Bay!

Joe: Inviting me?

Val: Beseeching you!

Joe: Week-end?

Val: Week-end!

Joe: Soon, soon?

Val: Soon, soon!

Joe: Must rush!

Val: Must totter!

Joe: Night, night!

Val: Night, night!

Joe: Darling, darling!

Val: Sweet, sweet!

They embrace, unclinch, and exeunt right and left as they entered.

Scholars will be fascinated

24
HEELS' PROGRESS

THEY are, of course, only a fragrant memory, and they were among the first to disappear in the great military snatch, so that names which once passed as currency in Ralph's and Walgreen's and Jack and Charlie's ended by illustrating and lending just the faintest glamour to the California regiments which were whipped together in the first years of the fighting forties. They were the Manhattan hall-room boys who had heeded Horace Greeley, the sports-coated emigrants to El Dorado, the dress-suit Okies who ornamented the beaches of Laguna, even as the beaches of Lucanan before the sealers came.

Probably not a social manifestation of any valiant consequence which will ever engage the attention of Charles and Mary Beard, as must the swifter runners in the caviar sweepstakes who ended clattering with platinum bangles at El Morocco and cabañas at the Surf Club at Miami Beach, the dress-suit Okies were the also-rans, the tidbits of passion, the gobbets of blackmail, and the paradigms of elegant shiftlessness who found it was easier to live for free in California than in Manhattan. Marion Davies gave less inhibited barn-raisings; the Coast Inn at Laguna had outside staircases to all the apartments; Bruz Fletcher sang "Night Flight to Reno" more swooningly in Icky Outhwaite's and Edie Hoffenstein's Club Bali in the County Strip in Hollywood. Don't ask where are they now, and, for Christ's sake, don't look around. There's one standing right behind you at the bar and looking thirsty, and he's a lieutenant in the Navy. Imagine!

In ever increasing quantities there emerged into the highly touted California sunlight members of a classification in the hierarchy of bumdom who never came to the attention of the railroad bulls or the smartly uniformed State Troopers, although they might tangle with the private guards of Bel Air and the ubiquitous plainclothesmen of the Los Angeles municipal police force. Their cars, like those of the Okies, were of the genus jaloppy, and their ambition was to live off the best that the devisings of nature and an easygoing public might provide. But here the resemblance ceased. For they were young men, all of them, most of them innocent of employment of any sort, none of them contaminated by physical toil. Their aged and spavined motors were spick-and-span, their attire the cheap imitations of beach and resort clothes now sold by every four-corners haberdasher in the nation; and in place of the bedsteads and washing paraphernalia of the emigrant farmers, their luggage included swimming and tennis clothes, an assortment of evening attire, phonographs and record magazines, radios, and other accoutrements of the life of leisure and pseudo-sophistication.

For these were the dress-suit Okies of California, the modern and American version of the remittance man of Kipling and English imperial times. They were the moochers de luxe, come to bum exclusively on the fat and the cream of the sunny land, come to live the lives of luxurious Rileys in the closely guarded preserves of wealth and class in Beverly Hills and similar havens of the haves. And for the most part they not only found what they were looking for, but were thanked for taking the handouts of caviar and champagne as no legitimate bum is ever thanked for wolfing a beef stew at a Los Angeles mission. California was filled with hostesses in need of week-end guests and film folks in search of personable and amusing companionship and satellites with cars to spare. The fashionable Okies who made good were thus enabled to carry on an existence swinging between near-destitution and windfalls, between lean week-days and fat week-ends. Keeping it up took work of a kind, but it was a kind that didn't make calluses on the palms, beyond those inflicted by a tennis racket, and hence was not in conflict with the code of gentlemanly loafing.

Not all the dinner-jacket drifters came overland from the corn lands of Iowa, the filling-stations of Texas, or the theatrical drugstores of Broadway by motor-car. They also patronized extensively the coach and tourist trains recently inaugurated by all the major transcontinental trunklines: the Union Pacific's Challengers, the super-swank, extra-fare coaches of the Santa Fé's El Capitans which made the same carded time between Chicago and Los Angeles as the Super Chiefs, and the tourist Pullmans of the Rock Island-Espee varnish hauls by way of Tucumcari. For the dress-suit Okie was not entirely destitute. He traveled, to be sure, on an absolute minimum of cash outlay derived from a variety of sources, and he figured the angles of free living with an adventurer's acuteness. But his scheme of things was predicated on getting not the third-rate things of life, the bare necessities, for nothing, but instead the very best things, the de luxe devisings of the world, at a minimum outlay of effort backed up by all his resources of person and personality. His success, therefore, depended much on appearances, on personal fastidiousness and the imitation of smart attire, and he had to have at least a smattering of knowledge of the language and usage of restaurants, theaters, and night clubs. He might actually have come in contact with a few of the great, usually of the cinema world, but he had to speak familiarly and with a moderate amount of plausibility of all of them.

The dress-suit Okie's origin was as various as the variety of states, occupations, and social circumstances in existence. He might be a simple rustic who had saved one hundred dollars on the farm and was determined to make it his stake in the El Dorado of California's opulent life. He might be a sometime Manhattan glamour boy whose name was not unknown to the paragraphers and who had worn out the welcome signs on the better doormats of Newport, Palm Beach, and Miami, and was determined to start operations anew at Burlingame, Santa Barbara, or La Jolla. Or he might be an occasionally employed night-club entertainer, chorus boy, or bit player, a Fifty-second Street adventurer with friends in the films who had cottages at Laguna and would be glad of his company if he would pay his own way out and chip in on the domestic budget. Most successful of the West Coast Hall-room Boys were probably those in this last category. When put to it, they had enough friends, influence, and accredited standing to get short-time breaks in the film studios or in the curious jungle of Hollywood's night life. They might even have small incomes from home or savings from former jobs, and they had a genuine, if minor, professional standing which made it possible to drift amiably and opulently along with authentic celebrities.

There was, as has been suggested, no rule of thumb for the rise and eventual flowering of the dinner-jacket hobo. It may have been as shrouded in obscurity as that of any main-line bindlestiff who lives by making the grab-irons and dies when the gases get him in the tunnel at Santa Susana. Precisely the opposite was true of one well-known remittance lad of the late 'thirties—the son of a prominent actress whose distaste for his excesses and public exploits prompted her to pay him twenty-five dollars a week to keep out of whatever part of the world she might be working in. Of the then crop of snob-Okies in California, one was secretary to a San Francisco banker and had recently purchased himself a handsome annuity against the time when he would be tired of it all and want to retire to a cottage in the desert. Scores of attractive youths cruised the Strip in Hollywood with no other aim than being picked up for gin and "feelthy moving picture" parties in houses up the Canyon, which might happily be prolonged into week-end excursions to Long Beach or Laguna. Others were polite and mannerly fellows, noted for their piano playing or dancing or articulate conversation, who added an atmosphere of cultivation and good breeding to the dinner tables of film stars themselves not noted for either.

The life cycle of the Forty-fifth Street–Sunset Boulevard black-tie drifter was a study of current American values that should fascinate the student of social and economic evolution. It was defined and conditioned by a series of indexes whose clarity rivaled that of route markings on U.S. highways and which were then recognizable to every amateur of the fantastic.

From Walgreen's theatrical drugstore to Ralph's minor stage rendezvous on Forty-fifth Street and Reilly's ushers' and chorus boys' hangout on Fifty-second opposite the practically moribund Tony's, were the initial steps on the ladder to a contract with Paramount. From Ralph's to Sardi's and from Sardi's to Jack and Charlie's was the course of recognition and honors, just as the progress of a scholar moves from baccalaureate to master's degree, to doctorate and the honorary hoods, capes and ermine of knowledge, ending with the Trice-Mage glory of the Sorbonne, whose Hollywood equivalent was a front table at Ciro's. And with each step in advancement there was visible and even tangible an appreciation in juvenile pretentiousness and snobbishness and chi-chi which was to have its ultimate fulfilment, when the wheel had come full circle, behind the necktie counter at Desmond's in Los Angeles or behind the pumps in some Wilshire Boulevard filling-station.

In the Walgreen's stage of evolution, the pre-Cambrian era of glamour boy geology, he was a naïve and penurious nonentity, stage-struck not for the sake of the stage but for the contacts it might bring, an amiable heel and bait for all the town's party-giving social wolves and wolverines. By the time he had achieved Ralph's (the Paleozoic era) he had acquired the beginnings of arrogance and a fine patina of chorus-girl bitchery. By the time he was exchanging witticisms with Renée at Sardi's, he was sporting a large but very pale star-sapphire ring, and experienced observers knew that he was lost to all reason and that his major occupation was giving what Broadway's first press agent, Dick Maney, calls the double brush-off to the friends who had known him in the Walgreen days and let him sleep on their sofas when the landlady had slipped him a French key. The final stage in the New York chapter of heel's progress was when he acquired his first opera hat, started talking champagne vintages with Philip, the waiter captain at "21," and attending first nights in such a flurry of bowing and smirking and boyish winsomeness as often enough provided a better show than that across the footlights. By this time he had had bit parts in two shows, struck up an acquaintance with Bernie Hart, and discarded so many friends of the Reilly's days that his conversation, to hear him tell it, was limited to members of the rarefied circle of Cole Porter, Vinton Freedley, and Jack Warner.

The translation of the wonder boy from the perfumed purlieus of Monte Carlo and El Morocco, where he appeared invariably in the capacity of guest, to the status of authentic dress-suit Okie at a ringside table at Slapsy Maxy's might be accomplished in several ways. A short-term option might be taken on his professional services by one of the studios, in which case his departure, via drawing-rooms on the Century and Chief, was something fearful and wonderful to behold and combined the best features of a show window at Abercrombie and Fitch's and a production number from *Aïda*. Or he might be invited west as a houseguest in one of the innumerable villas of Beverly Hills, an anabasis which he undertook with a smug reticence suggestive of secret and not-yet-to-be-revealed agreements with Darryl Zanuck or Mr. De Mille. Or, he might simply pool his resources with two or three lads in similar case, tell his friends he'd let them know when he had an address, and set forth in the transcontinental assurance that at the other end of U. S. No. 66 there lay a wonderful, wonderful farrago of swimming pools, sunshine, collations of caviar and lobster aspic, week-ends at Palm Springs, and *la vie* and *l'amour* in their every manifold form, all of them practically free. And as a matter of fact, he was right.

The time which elapsed before the three types of voyagers west achieved the identical rating as manicured moochers depended only upon the longevity of the studio's option upon the first in the category. For three months, for six or for a year, he might wax sassy, though not physically fat, on all the devisings of his agent's imagination. The primary requisites were a flock of sports clothes from Jack Bell in Vine Street, a bucket-seat sports roadster of livid design, complete with prop police dog and polo mallets, a villa of proportions far in excess of his requirements in the fashionable real estate development of the moment, and Thursday (maid's night out) appearances at Dave Chasen's. When, as was inevitable, the studio declined to renew its option, the men came for the piano and the dealer put the snatch on the roadster; then the midnight chimes struck for Cinderella, and he joined the other boys who were panting for an invitation to one of Mrs. Basil Rathbone's celebratedly hospitable levees.

Once located amid the swimming-pool-and-swami civilization, the polo-coat Okie could never afford to be entirely destitute. Such basic considerations as rent, breakfast, laundry, valeting, and transportation, as well as an occasional gesture in the direction of reaching for a bar check just for the sake of appearances, presupposed a certain amount of out-of-pocket expenditure, except in the cases of youths actually in the paid possession of the opulent elderly, a comparatively rare manifestation. In order to assure this necessary minimum of currency, there were a variety of jobs, some part-time, none too exacting of hours, at his disposal: bit parts in the studios; hoofing and hollering, if he possessed the talent, in the night clubs; serving, if he had a name and friends, as shill for restaurants and hot spots; acting as runner for Hollywood tailors (usually here the compensation was in gaudy raiment rather than in cash); selling the classic neckties at Desmond's; working behind the counter at drive-ins; selling automobiles on commission; acting as secretary, courier, and general *fidus Achates* to established actors and executives; and, of course, interior decorating.

If he was really adroit, knew his angles, and was a young man of imagination and presence, a Sunset Boule-

He wanted the best for a minimum outlay

vard drifter with twenty-five dollars a week in his kick
and a convenient absence of any suspicions of personal
morality could live on a scale that would set him back
eight or ten times as much if he actually paid for the
Scotch, the Buicks, the cover charges at Perino's Sky
Room, and week-end excursions to the better beach
houses at Santa Barbara. As has been remarked before,
the philosophy of the calling consisted of looking not
for a little for nothing, so much as for the works for
a minimum outlay.

Less exotic entertainment, but just as ample in vita-
mins, calories, and alcoholic content, was available at
the hands of hostesses who had become authentic Hollywood institutions; and the Boxcar Bennies and Bozo

Texinos of Marmont Lane and the smarter avenues of Beverly Hills glittered and did themselves handsomely at the seemingly perpetual lunches and cocktail parties of Connie Bennett, the Countess Dorothy di Frasso, and Mrs. Frank Borzage. The *crème de la crème Yvette* of the Hall-room Boys might even find themselves bidden to the small but elaborate dinners of Hollywood's most perceptive gourmet, Mrs. Samuel Hoffenstein. The starred performers at the boards of these hospitable loaves-and-fishes experts were, of course, Names of Consequence, but around the edges of the assembled chivalry was discernible a fine froth, as of tulle, of hungry and handsome juveniles who went home only to reappear in more splendid and formal attire the moment their hostess suggested a prowl of the dinner resorts of the Strip or excursion on the premises of Don the Original Beachcomber.

For the more ingenuous, to whom the elaborate charades and plaisances of Hollywood and Malibu Beach held infrequent charms, there were the naïve delights (or not so naïve, if one desired) of the innumerable dim-lit bistros of Hollywood Boulevard; of free passes to previews, which were scattered like double-feature chaff by studio press agents; and of sun bathing and dunking the body at Santa Monica Beach, happily available by trolley if motor transport was not forthcoming.

Whatever might be his dish of tea, California in general and Los Angeles in particular was the Big Rock Candy Mountain of the tail-coated hobo. The simple life of sun-tan, swimming, sleep, and sneak previews on next to nothing was there for the shiftless or indifferent hedonist. The convertible coupés, the double magnums of Clicquot, the Palm Springs villas, and the fascinating games they played at Al Wirtheimer's Dunes Club were available for the boys with the toothpaste smile, the patter, and the wherewithal to keep the hair and finger-nails gleaming and to ransom the evening linen from the Chinaman with a reasonable degree of regularity. Step right up, brother, and have a try; two bits gets you ten dollars! And, amazingly enough, once upon a time, long, long ago, it did!

25

RIGADOON OF CONFUSIONS

A REPORTER REMEMBERS: The year that Dorothy Gish and Tipton Blish who employed a Javanese servant named Nish, all lived in the same entry of the same apartment house, Beekman Terrace, and the confusion that resulted therefrom. Blish, being a less consequential tenant than Miss Gish, finally withdrew with Nish.

⁕

The fabulous dinners of the late Albert Keller, managing director of the Ritz, at which Bob Davis, Karl K. Kitchen, Odd McIntyre, and I used to sit up all night over the stewpot devisings of Louis Diat, the chef, while I, a juvenile, listened bug-eyed to the anecdotes and fabrications of the mighty word painters.

⁕

The time when Scudder Middleton, newly elected to the Players Club, found Reggie Birch, artist-creator of Little Lord Fauntleroy, leaning against the bar in a 4 A.M. trance and called for John, the night porter who was sweeping the premises, to help get the great man upstairs and to bed. "'At's all right, Mr. Middleton," said John soothingly to the agitated Scudder, who evidently feared Birch was about to be relegated to the dust bin. "I allus sweeps around him!"

*

The first evening dimout of the war, when there was a Broadway opening of consequence with all the notables lighting matches to see if they were getting into the Astor Bar, and Sardi's waiters, forethoughtfully armed by their employer with flash torches, escorting the blind and thirsty across Forty-fifth Street to his restaurant.

*

My amazement once when driving through the California night and pausing for gas at Fresno to discover across the street a complete replica El Morocco, a facsimile in every detail of zebra stripes, palm trees, and Foreign Legion doorman. The proprietor had purchased the entire décor once when Perona was redecorating.

*

The solid brick fireplace and three feet of masonry chimney, all mounted on a truck, which are wheeled into private dining-rooms at the Yale Club at ushers' dinners to smash glasses in when toasts are drunk and then solemnly wheeled out again by housefootmen.

*

Condé Nast's parties, where the guests were recruited from extremely arbitrary lists from the worlds of music, theater, French politics, and such, and the outraged

Sardi provided a light in the darkness

dismay of Muriel Draper on one occasion. "Imagine!" she said. "It was an evening party, and Condé had in all the afternoon people!"

✳

William Morris Houghton's recollection of meeting the great James Huneker, years ago, at a hangout called Knieram's Eats and Pilsener Sanitarium, favored by old *World* staffmen, and Huneker's acknowledgment of the introduction: "Always glad to meet a reporter, Mr. Houghton, once a newspaperman always a whore!" Henry Cabot Lodge, Jr., who was standing by in Bleeck's when Houghton told the story, was livid. "Why, Bill," he snorted in editorial dismay. "If I believed that I'd never have joined the profession!"

✳

Sherman Hoyt, who once when sailing a tiny sloop in the races from New London to Bermuda came upon the huge *Monarch of Bermuda* stopped in mid-ocean for engine repairs. A flutter of signal flags appeared at Hoyt's masthead, and there was a great rushing around of brass hats on the *Monarch's* bridge to decipher the message. Finally it was decoded to read: "Can I be of any assistance?"

✳

The platinum chain and ear clips retailing for two hundred and fifty dollars which Paul Flato, once fashionable jeweler to the faubourgs, ran up during the deepest years of the depression for the purpose of keeping spaniels' ears out of their dogfood.

✳

My fortunate encounter, once, aboard the stream-liner *City of San Francisco* during a particularly drastic wartime shortage of meat and good liquor, with Eugene Myer, publisher of the Washington *Post,* who had two drawing-rooms in the Pullman "Chinatown": one for himself and one filled with steak and cases of champagne destined to relieve suffering among Pacific coast friends.

✳

The time Bruce Cabot and I, in Reno on a tear, found ourselves in a notable deadfall, the Dog House or some such, where we were being trimmed to our last shinplaster at roulette. Suddenly the house started paying off, and the croupier, in a panic, yelled for the house carpenter: "Hey, Charlie, hurry over to table nine! The wheel's on the fritz and the customers are winning!"

✳

Walking down Fifth Avenue with Vincent Youmans, the composer, whose family for generations before him had been well-known manufacturers of men's hats. At Fifty-second Street Youmans paused to point out the site of his ancestral business, now occupied by expensive and fashionable jewelry shops, interior decorators, and furriers. "Squatters!" he snarled.

✳

The perfumed elevators in the Ritz Carlton, piloted by flunkies in court tailcoats and knee breeches. For years I imagined the perfume was an added elegance of life, until I discovered it was incidental to a disinfectant.

✳

The luncheon party I gave for Paul Smith, publisher of the San Francisco *Chronicle,* Herb Caen, its columnist, and Bob Hanley, in a Goodyear blimp over San Francisco, where we threw the eggshells and other incidentals down on Mr. Hearst's elegant San Simeon estate.

✳

The opening night, years ago, of Peter Arno's dramatic nonesuch, *Here Goes the Bride,* a dingus allegedly based on his own Reno experiences in which he engaged in a slight shooting with Cornelius Vanderbilt, Jr. The show was such a terrible bust that, although Jock Whitney had taken over the Starlight Roof of the Waldorf for a celebration afterward, nobody but the hard-boiled press had the nerve to show up. Fifteen or twenty reporters did away with all the caviar, cigars, and champagne intended for a hundred-odd invitees.

✳

The costly Lagonda motor-car once possessed by Peter Moon, the Chicago playboy, which had three or four speeds backward as well as four or five forward gears. Peter received such frequent summonses for traffic and speed-regulation infringements that he had a basket hung outside the driver's door to receive police papers, like a postbox.

✳

Amon Carter, the Fort Worth publisher and banker, is celebrated for his generosity. Once, when on safari in Texas, I visited his Shady Oak Farm and admired his herd of long horn steers, the last in existence, he turned ingenuously and remarked: "Let me send you one!"

✳

Katharine Brush's battery of twelve portable type-writers ranged around a huge desk where she follows her trade of beautiful letters. Each is a different color, to suit the lady novelist's mood.

✳

The boisterous and uninhibited quality of Robert Benchley's horse laugh at first nights in the theater contrasted with his sober and domesticated mien at Sunday luncheon with his family at the Plaza.

✳

The elaborate Russian Easter parties once given by Valentina Schlee, where each of the guests used to get a china egg which had originally been given away at one of the Czar's parties.

✳

The late Tom Mix, leaning against the bar of the Riverside Hotel in Reno and telling me about his first emergence to fame and fortune by way of the films many years ago. As a cow hand he had always had a hanker for de luxe elegances of living and, when he was at last able to indulge it, he took with him to Hollywood as his valet, courier and Fidus Achates, an old sidekick from the ranges. To be sure they always addressed each other by their first names, drank in the same saloons and got in fist fights with each other, but, anyway Mix had a valet at last. He outfitted the ex-puncher with seven suits of livery, one for each day in the week, which Spike wore with high heeled boots and spurs for a panache. So that nobody would underestimate his magnificence or imagine for a minute that the elevated cow hand was possessed of but one uniform, Mix had run up for him seven caps with the legend across the front, in gold letters: "Tom Mix, Monday," "Tom Mix, Tuesday," etc. Everyone, Mix recalled, was vastly impressed with such chic.

✳

The time in the Ritz Bar in Paris when I introduced Prince Mike Romanoff (Harry Gerguson) to the authentic Prince Michael Romanoff, the accomplished musician, and Prince Mike leveled an accusatory finger at the real Michael and shouted, "This man is an impostor. Throw him out!"

✳

The Easter Parade on Fifth Avenue in which I appeared on the top of a horse-drawn coach with Ethel Merman, Monty Woolley, Bert Lahr, and Peggy LeBoutillier Williams on such a sub-zero day that everybody had to drink brandy out of a bottle to keep from freezing to death then and there. Woolley dropped the bottle, and it fell to the pavement with a hideous crash right in front of St. Patrick's Cathedral.

✳

The days when, at the first fall of snow or even a suspicion of it, I used to hire Pat Rafferty's sleigh off the Plaza cabrank and race Major William Kennelly, president of the N.Y.A.C., who owned his own cutter, for a magnum of champagne in Central Park. Since the gallant Major always raced from the Athletic Club in Fifty-ninth Street to the Sheepfold on the Green, and since I invariably raced from the Madison in Fifty-eighth Street to the Central Park Casino, we both, almost inevitably, won and were presented with magnums of wine by the managements, grateful for the publicity and good-old-days atmosphere.

* *

The wedding of Tony Williams, the social tailor to New York's bright young men, where I served as head usher and every one of the twelve groomsmen wore a different arrangement of morning clothes. So did the attendants of the bride, whose father, George LeBoutillier, was president of Best and Company. At the reception afterward, Howard Davis, business manager of the *Herald Tribune*, was heard to address Mr. LeBoutillier. "George," he queried, "however are you going to get those dresses off those girls, get them dry cleaned and back in the show windows by the time you open for business to-morrow morning?"

* *

The evening, a short time ago, when David Cowles, proprietor of the Penquin, a smart and prosperous little Manhattan restaurant located in what had once been Cobina Wright's home, was forced to shut up shop by reason of the scarcity of taxi transport. He phoned all his personal friends with the urgent exhortation: "Drop whatever you're doing, whatever it may be, and hurry over. I'm closing tonight and we have to empty the cellar before the directors hear about it!" The town wasn't the same for a week.

* *

Such personal knickknacks as the Cartier champagne swizzle of solid platinum worn by Alfred Barton on his watch-chain; George Buchanan Fife's inevitable batwing collar and butterfly bow tie; the crimson-satin-lined opera cloak of H. T. Parker of the lamented Boston *Evening Transcript;* photographer Howard Cagle's evening studs of diamonds cut to resemble flash bulbs.

✳

The occasion when Wolcott Gibbs of the *New Yorker* set fire to himself smoking in bed and the night operator of his apartment house refused to call the fire department, thinking his frantic call was a practical joke.

✳

The moment when, ten minutes after the conclusion of the radio broadcast, December 7, 1941, my roommate reached for his hat and said: "Are the Navy recruiting offices open on Sunday?"

✳

Finding myself in the steam room in the Finnish bath at Charlie Farrell's Racquet Club at Palm Springs with Boris Karloff and Peter Lorre at the same time and wondering what my chances were of escaping alive.

✳

The Sunday afternoon in mid-August in Denver that Evalyn Walsh McLean took it into her head to give a dinner party of fantastic proportions the same evening at the Brown Palace Hotel, and how, six hours later, we sat down to a full-dress, white-tie turnout with two name bands, enormous ice elephants full of fresh caviar, quadruple bottles of Bollinger '26, roast Mexican quail and the *crème de la crème d'Isigny* of Denver society. Only the Brown Palace and only Evie McLean could contrive such magnificence.

✳

The dinner party arranged at the Savoy Plaza by André Simon for the organization of the American chapter of the Wine and Food Society, at which the master swooned when he discovered the management had laid a single train of orchids down the center of the long table. "Throw wide the windows!" he cried. "Air the rooms! Is the bouquet of my wines to have to conflict with these stinking flowers?"

✳

Driving one night through the desolate San Jacinto Mountains of California and discovering, miles from the nearest town or even filling-station, a handsomely appointed and brightly lighted saloon whose wine list, liquor shelves, and general setup would have done credit to any metropolitan midst. "How," I inquired, "do you manage to support such a tony dump so far from any town?" "Oh," explained the barkeep, "we open up just before the health farm up the road a ways lets the inmates out for the evening!"

✳

The spun-platinum blades of straw Mrs. S. Stanwood Menken had run up by Tiffany to wear in her hair at a costume ball where she was to appear dressed as a simple country maiden.

✳

Lunchtime at Jack and Charlie's on December 9, 1941, a few minutes after some Army goon, later cashiered, had announced over the radio that German airraiders were going to bomb the city within the hour. All the most fashionable folk, the Vincent Astors, Mrs. Larry Tibbett, Dwight Deere Wiman, and the society paragraphers jammed the premises in their newest and fanciest rigs, sure that the photographers would be present and desirous of being blown to bits in their best Daché bonnets and smartest clothes.

✳

Covering the opening of *Virginia City* at Virginia City, Nevada, I was typing a wire story in the Western Union office when the report arrived that Tite's Opera House had fallen in and that scores of celebrities were killed or maimed. Knowing that Howard Barnes from my own paper was in the audience, I hastily cut my story to advise the telegraph desk in New York to get his obituary out of the files and dashed up Eureka Street, only pausing in the Crystal Chandelier Saloon to fortify myself against the horrors I should encounter at the scene of desolation. To my inestimable relief, there was Barnes hoisting a hod of red ruin with Johnny Harkins of Paramount. The roof of Tite's had, to be sure, fallen in, but ten minutes after the close of the performance, and there had been nobody in the building.

✳

The incredible and hair-raising profanity of Richard Maney, the press agent, whose vocabulary is innocent of any least curse word or obscenity but derives its effectiveness entirely from the sonorous rhythms of Elizabethan English.

✳

The first time I ever had a highball in a London pub and the barmaid inquired would I have "splash or polly, please" with my whisky? Having no slightest knowledge of the circumstance that she wanted to know if I wished seltzer or Apollinaris water, I timidly allowed that I'd like a little of both, if I might! I can still hear the homeric laughter of the other customers.

✳

The Webster Hall brawls engineered by Cynthia White, the last of the Greenwich Bohemians, now departed these parts, but once the roughest parties in town, from which any one was lucky to emerge with all his teeth and a complete scalp.

✳

The most wistful souvenir of the old West, I have always thought, is the Hotel de Paris, built and for many years run by "French Louis" du Puy, in the silver boom town of Georgetown, in Colorado, high in the hills above Denver. Haunted by the ghost of French Louis, who first brought fine food and wines to the mining-towns in 1875, it stands to this day, intact in Georgetown's Alpine street, a museum of mirrors and etchings, statues, ormolu, fountains, Limoges china, and fragrant souvenirs of sheep's feet in sauce soubise, trout portugaise, and other novelties of a frontier time. Of all the relics of all the ghost towns of Colorado, it is the most incongruous, most pathetic, most lonely, with the desolate hills rising behind its statued façade and its register a tally of the great names of the storied and wonderful West.

✳

The time when, for some first night or other, I squired Libby Holman on the town only to discover that in the course of the evening she had worn three differently and progressively more costly fur wraps. The first, a simple mink, she discarded at the Colony in favor of something in ermine, which she wore to the theater and as far as Monte Carlo, where she picked up a flock of wonderful sables, some of them, I thought alive. Her maid kept going ahead and planting them in case she got tired of what she was at the moment wearing.

✳

Banker Rufus Dawes, at the opening of the Streets of Paris at the Chicago World's Fair, in tails and an opera hat from which descended trailers of woven orchids, the relic of some elaborate lady's corsage.

✳

Belle Livingstone's Fifty-eighth Street Country Club, a prohibition deadfall, where she contrived to have two regular precinct officers in uniform inside the doorway to keep out unwanted Federal agents.

✳

Pausing for a beer one morning at the Jackhammer Café, a celebratedly hard-boiled desert cabaret in Indio, California, about a million miles from nowhere, to find the band, which consisted of five hat-in-hand college boys who had obviously got the bounceroo the night before, asking for their job back. I was just in time to hear the proprietor, obviously a desert Chesterfield, admonish them: "All right, you Joes can have the job back, but in future no throwing your empty whisky pints at the customers on the dance floor. Somebody might get hurt, you see, and besides, it's rude!"

✳

The radio broadcast with George Jessel, whose sponsor was a nationally promoted hair restorer. It was in the old Broadway Theater in front of hundreds of leering goons in free seats, and just as Jessel went to town on the commercial and was shouting into the microphone that the restorer would make bald pates blossom like a fragrant garden, his wig fell forward over his nose and very effectively gagged him.

✳

The waiters' strike which established John and Jerrold Krimsky and myself as the proprietors of a modest Broadway success. When we opened at the American Music Hall, of which we were the joint exploiters, with *Murder in the Old Red Barn* in 1936, the night of our grand, gala, super for-free première at this dramatic boozing kennel, our entire staff of waiters walked out in a union huff. The regular servitors and barkeeps had been instructed to keep the free strong waters within reason, at least until the reviewers had had a chance to see the show, but when the Brothers Krimsky, Richard Maney, our press agent, Angela Krimsky, and I were forced to start rushing drinks for our guests, all restraint vanished in the ensuing confusion. So happily bemused were the reporters by the time they came to write their notices that the defects of the dramatic nonesuch fled their minds and we got universal rave reviews.

✳

At one of Evalyn Walsh McLean's dinners at her old Friendship in Wisconsin Avenue in Washington, Joseph Hergesheimer's telling me he was working on his autobiography. There was to be no need of an index since there wasn't going to be a single name of any other person mentioned. Only Joseph Hergesheimer.

＊

The luncheon given me in the State Suite of the Palace Hotel in San Francisco on the celebrated Palace solid gold plate the first year of the Golden Gate Fair. There were twenty guests, mostly Crockers and Camerons, twenty house footmen, twenty men from the Val O'Farrell Detective Agency to watch the waiters, two barkeeps, a wine steward, two hotel executives, and four waiter captains. The gold service got back to the vaults of the Bank of America practically intact.

＊

The mid-continent chic and splendor which attends the first nights every summer (suspended during the war years) at Central City, the Colorado ghost town high in the Rockies above Denver, where, in a midst that once knew Haw Tabor, Horace Greeley, General Grant, Modjeska, Sarah Bernhardt and Edwin Booth, the chivalry of Colorado goes all out for foolish luxe revivals at the old Opera House. In the lonely ravine above the Boston Mine, where once prospectors shoved pokes of gold across the bars of the Silver Coin Saloon and the Teller House, each year now there are imported motor-cars, formal evening attire, gowns from I. Magnin and Hattie Carnegie, truffled foie gras, and house servants forwarded from Denver for the occasion, and the photographers' speed guns flicker where frontier-model six-guns were once accustomed currency. Central City nights probably present the most dramatic

contrast in America between a setting of lonely wonder
and the luxurious devisings of urban existence.

✳

The fashion show at Elizabeth Hawes', whose mod-
ernistic shop possessed solid glass doors devoid of frames.
So eager was a rival bonnet foundryman, John Frederics,
to attend an evening salon at Miss Hawes' one dimmed-
out night that he walked directly through the door without opening it and arrived covered with shards of heavy
glass, but undismayed, to tumultuous applause from the
assembled chivalry.

✳

Once, at a public luncheon in San Francisco, sitting
at the speakers' table with Paul Smith, manager of the
Chronicle, on whose other hand was Dale Carnegie.
There being a flock of orators, each of us was limited to
a minute, but not Carnegie, who, bent on making
friends and influencing people, spoke on endlessly.
Smith, as chairman of the occasion, tugged at his coat-
tails, pointed to the face of his watch, cleared his throat,
nudged the speaker's knee, all to no avail. Carnegie
talked on and on, bewitched and bemused by his own
forensics. Finally, after fifteen or twenty minutes, Smith
muttered: "I fix," and left the table. A few moments
later half a dozen waiters filed in and sat down at vacant
places at the reporters' table, directly below the speaker.
"Look," croaked Smith in a stage whisper, pulling Carnegie's coat and pointing to the boiled shirt-fronts on
the waiters. "People coming in for dinner!" Carnegie
stepped down.

26

WHO AM I?

I F life in Manhattan takes on at times, for other parts of the national countryside, aspects of other-world existence at once fantastic and frightening, and if its inhabitants assume a variety of characteristics, inherited and acquired, never yet catalogued by science, part of the credit, at least, may be passed on to the paragraphers and syndicated columnists who chronicle its more gaudy personal doings. Cause and result have become obscured in the evolution of the national consciousness, but if to-day's reporters waltz up a dream world between the East River and the North which is utterly unrecognizable to the inhabitants of New York itself, it is frequently enough because that is what the reading public west of the Hudson requires of them through its agents, the managing editors of local newspapers, and no managing editor has ever yet been wrong where a syndicated writer was concerned. Whether the legend of fantasy that has engulfed New York had its origin with O. Henry or Odd McIntyre or Dion Boucicault is neither here nor there. It is established and clearly defined in the suburban mind, a fixed and immutable concept, to tamper with which is professional death.

By the same token, most New Yorkers who rate mention in columns and paragraphs usually have a hard time recognizing themselves when they encounter an entirely foreign fellow in the morning shaving mirror. The personage with a name that makes what passes for news is subject to strange confusions and contradictions which eventually may lead to a city entirely populated by schizophrenics. The writer, for example, always has to look twice in a mirror before he can recognize in the commonplace image that presents itself a guy who, at that very red-hot moment, is at once a scoundrel of Homeric proportions and a white knight of beautiful letters, is simultaneously situated on a stool at the Stork Club and lying in a gutter in the Strip in Hollywood, who synchronously and at once is fabulously affluent and in the hands of the Federal dogberries for tax arrears, and is at one and the same time a fop of exquisite proportions and a shiftless oaf in baggy pants from whom the late Heywood Broun would have recoiled as from a street accident.

Within a period of a few years he has variously discovered himself, through the agency of Romeike's clipping bureau, to have inherited several million dollars, to be stark dead by his own impetuous hand, to be a member, paid up and in good standing, of the Cliveden set, whatever that may be; to be in Washington and to be flying a pursuit plane or some such for the R. A. F. There are, of course, incidental confusions, such as that he invariably sleeps in a top hat, brushes his teeth in a

properly chilled Chablis, and dines simultaneously every
night at Jack and Charlie's, the Colony, the Pump
Room in Chicago, and the Golden Pheasant in Dallas,
Texas. The circumstances that he is still in senile, perhaps, yet animate circulation, that the sheriff's men are
after him for debt, that he has not the foggiest notion
of the doings of the selectmen in his own native Wake-
field, Mass., let alone national affairs, that he is in ab-
ject terror of flying machines and his sole military
experience has been the occasional passing of Banner-
man's Island Arsenal on the way to Albany, just don't
count. The best he can do is view the reality of his
existence and remark: "A poor virgin, Sir, an ill-fav-
ored thing, Sir, but mine own."

(2)